THE SPEED OF LOVE

AN EXPLORATION OF CHRISTIAN FAITHFULNESS IN A TECHNOLOGICAL WORLD

DAVID P. YOUNG

ISBN 0-377-00159-7
Editorial Offices: 475 Riverside Drive, Room 772, New York, NY 10115
Distribution Offices: P.O. Box 37844, Cincinnati, OH 45237
Copyright © 1986 Friendship Press, Inc.
Printed in the United States of America

DEDICATION

To the continuing struggle, as evident in the
exchange between Anpao, a Native American
equivalent to the Greek Homer, and an old, old
Indian man.

Anpao: "Nothing makes sense if everything
       has to end."

Old Man: "No, the wonder is that it has
       happened at all."

May we ever find the strength to be faithful
to that wonder. . .so that our serving is to the
presence of truth, and not comfort.

"The gift must always move"

ACKNOWLEDGEMENTS

Ideas begin in secret places. And when they show themselves and begin to grow into fullness they often leave long trails of encounters. So it has been with this book. As best as I can recollect, the idea for a collection of thoughts and images on pioneering a new technological/value future found me in the mid-1970's. There is no need to revisit the many steps along the way. However, there is a need to acknowledge my deep debt to the many persons who inspired and advised me. Any problems of wrongheadedness or misguided direction are solely mine. I have had the best help anyone could ask for.

So my deepest thanks to:

• friends at Central Philippine University in Iloilo City, Philippines who helped in 1977-79: Gus Pulido, Elma Herradura, Johnny Gumban, Intoy Ganchore, Becky Carman and John Turner (forgive my saving space in naming only a few),

• to friends who helped by commenting on drafts of this material: Robert Miller, Diane Kirkpatrick, Carlisle Harvard, Mary Lemmenes, Don Nead, Jack Sadler, Bob Grey, Pam Rhodes, Alastair Scougal and John Turner;

• to three singled out for special accolade: Sara Juengst, whose enthusiasm and vision got me into this particular project and who was a firm but friendly critic all along the way, Mark Davis, mentor/collaborator from way back who challenged both my manner of expression and my ideas and Rosita Bermudez, who coaxed draft after draft through my innumerable changes, but more importantly, who typed and discussed at the same time, always forcing me not to be afraid to listen to my inner thoughts;

• to Yvonne Roberts, who not only helped occasionally with typing but who also patiently attended to my normal work when I was off writing;

• to my wife, Sweet, and children Nancy, David, Jr., Laura, Emily and Cameron, who too often saw me disappear to my typewriter and not-to-be-disturbed moods, but especially to Sweet, who often stopped her quilting in order to listen to and comment on my struggles to find the right word or image;

　• to Nadine Hundertmark, who gave steady editorial support and advice that kept my focus on creativity and not panic;

　• and lastly, to the constant presence of experiences with the poor in over thirty countries, experiences that have never loosened their grip on me as I attempt to do what I can to share their dignity and their need.

CONTENTS

Note: Please insert this filmography in the Leaders' Guide "The Speed of Love."

FILMOGRAPHY
TECHNOLOGY IN TENSION WITH HUMAN VALUES

I. PRIMARY RESOURCES

Global Village. 26 minutes. 16mm film; ½" VHS and Beta video.

India, a developing nation with massive numbers of people living primarily in remote villages is making significant moves to use new forms of communications technology to serve the needs of the country. Satellites, computers, television productions are seen as the means by which the country can improve its transportation system, telephones, illiteracy and general education. This program takes a careful look at the innovations and potential impact upon the people.

Produced by World Association for Christian Communication, 1985. Rental from denominational resource centers or EcuFilm, (800) 251-4091, 810 Twelfth Ave. S., Nashville, TN 37203. Rental $25.00 for film, $15.00 for video.

II. OTHER RESOURCES

Technology in Dialogue with Human Values. 30 minutes. ½" VHS and Beta video.

The computer has become nearly omnipresent in the classrooms and other educational settings, and thus offers a paradigm of how technology affects interaction. In this CBS special program scientists, psychologists, and clergy debate the impact of the computer and how it will shape our future perceptions of ourselves. MIT's Sherry Turkel: "the computer can offer the illusion of companionship without the demands of friendship or the dangers of intimacy." Episcopal rector Fred Burnham: "it is an instrument of power — what do we do with it?" Engineering professor Judah Schwartz: "much use of computers is mindless."

Produced by CBS television, 1985. Rental from denominational resource centers or EcuFilm, (800) 251-4091. Rental $25.00.

Hard Choices: The Biomedical Challenges. 60 minutes. ½" VHS and Beta video.

The new moral and ethical dilemmas which have been created by our rapidly increasing knowledge and abilities are addressed in this program hosted by ABC TV's George Will — especially in the areas of the creation, restructuring, and prolongation of human life. A symposium of medical and religious thinkers responds to experts Alexander Capron, professor of law, medicine and public policy at University of Southern California; Leon Kass, professor of the liberal arts of human biology at the University of Chicago; and William F. May, professor of Christian ethics, Georgetown University.

Produced by ABC News, 1985. Rental from EcuFilm, (800) 251-4091. Rental $30.00.

Adult Learning: James Botkin. 45 minutes. ½" VHS and Beta Video.

Botkin takes a global perspective to identify the impact technology is having upon our lives and our methods of learning. He predicts that the "information society" will rapidly become the "bio-society" and then the "materials science society." This program concentrates on the implications of such technological impact upon adult learning, particularly for the church.

Produced by United Methodist Church, 1984. Rental $20.00 and Sale $39.00 from EcuFilm (800) 251-4091 or denominational resource centers.

High Tech: Dream or Nightmare? 60 minutes. ½" VHS and Beta video.

Walter Cronkite examines the impact of the high-tech revolution on the American work force today and what might be expected for the future. The high-tech revolution has led to the creation of boom towns like those in Silicon Valley, California, where high production has generated high employment and considerable prosperity. But tens of thousands of other workers are not reaping benefits from the high-tech dream. Instead, the computer age is making their skills obsolete, their jobs are being taken over by machines or eliminated completely. Their security is threatened, their future, uncertain.

Produced by CBS News, 1984. Rental from Carousel Films, 241 E. 34th St., New York NY 10016 (212) 683-1660. Rental $75.00.

Homo Homini/Acceleration. 11 minutes. 16mm film.

A deeply religious inquiry into where we are and where we are going in our world serves as a discussion starter for groups considering the impact of technology on life. Even though these films are several years old, they address the theme well.

Produced by World Council of Churches, 1968. Rental from denominational resource centers or EcuFilm (800) 251-4091. Rental $15.00

Future Shock. 42 minutes. 16mm film.

Based on Alvin Toffler's best seller by the same title, the film depicts the pressures of modern industry and technology which shape contemporary culture. The possibilities of science, both good and bad, force humanity to reconsider issues of morality, ethics and religion.

Produced by CRM/McGraw-Hill Films, 1973. Rental $70.00 from McGraw-Hill Films, Box 641, Del Mar, CA 92014 (619) 453-5000 or rental $35.00 from EcuFilm (800) 251-4091.

INTRODUCTION

LOVE HAS ITS SPEED

This is more a conversation than a book. It is a conversation about the direction of the human use of technology, how that use relates to our values and to our search for faithfulness to God's persistent breaking through into our lives. The essays that start this conversation are a collage of ideas about technology, values and faith. They invite us to search the horizon called future for landmarks that mean we are doing something about that persistent breaking through.

In my own part of this conversation, I will be talking about some strange things, like the technology of manna, sin in relation to nuclear technologies, the subjective computer, changing ourselves into a new species and the necessity of mystery. I will talk about these things not to be strange or impertinent, but very seriously, because I am deeply troubled. I believe we have gone to sleep with regard to the potential hazards of our technology. One evidence of this lethargy is our indifference to pollution. Because we hear only sporadically about it, we are lulled into thinking that "someone" is taking care of it. Yet the global industrialization that churns out waste materials proceeds unimpeded. A second sign of our lethargy is spiritual: we are lulled into the faith that more powerful, more expensive military technology will make us more secure. On top of all this there is the deep tragedy of our having gone to sleep with regard to grave injustices to persons and to the planet.

These essays are not a collection of predictions about the future; they are, rather, a kind of sampler, an exercising of the future to take seriously the notion of pioneering in a new direction. With regard to technology, the pioneering image centers around how technology should relate to the poor. With regard to values, the pioneering image is the connection between quality and technological choices. With regard to faithfulness, the pioneering image is in

1

the question, "What is required of us by God?" The recurring question is not "What are we doing?" but, "What *should* we be doing?"

This conversation takes seriously what Dorothy says in *The Wizard of Oz*, "Toto, I've a feeling we're not in Kansas anymore." Our changing technology demands a serious look at the *values* that support it if we care at all about *faithfulness* to the choices of love and justice.

There are three interrelated parts to this conversation. Two make up this book: a series of essays and a discussion guide. The third is a companion book titled, *21st Century Pioneering: A Scrapbook of the Future*. The intent of these essays is to stimulate thinking; that of the discussion guide is to stimulate deciding; and the intent of the Scrapbook is to stimulate playing. The essays are not comprehensive analyses, but rather, are aimed at turning familiar thoughts toward new angles of reflection so that new thoughts can be generated. They have been written with the invitation of T. H. Huxley in mind: "Sit down before a fact like a little child, and be prepared to give up every preconceived notion, follow humbly wherever and to whatever abysses Nature leads, or you shall learn nothing."[1] The discussion guide is aimed at developing the motivation and resolve to make decisions of greater faithfulness to the presence of *shalom* (peace with justice) rather than of faithfulness to the automatic expectations of the technological way. The words of Isaiah 42:6 have been very much in mind in its preparation: "I, the Lord, have called you and given you power to see that justice is done on earth." The Scrapbook springs from the conviction that in our technological world, rational and pragmatic ideas get too much attention. To be complete persons who continue to grow and respond faithfully to the gospel, we require also playing—serious fooling around. As Khellog Albran expressed it in *The Profit*: "It is easier for a camel to go through the eye of a needle if it is lightly greased."[2] (Hmm. Do you grease the needle or the camel?)

The combined impact of these three interrelated parts is that they consider the potential of moral, ethical, spiritual, religious pioneering—pioneering that will revitalize our contemporary materialistic standards of progress and what is "good." They form an exploration of Christian faithfulness in a technological world.

As you begin this exploration; pause only for one more thought: that of speed. Kosuke Koyama wrote: "Love has its speed. It is an inner speed. It is a spiritual speed. It is a different kind of speed from the technological speed to which we are accustomed."[3] What we are about to embark upon in this conversation is the speed of technology, the speed of love and most important, how the two might better travel together.

"DID WE COME HERE TO LAUGH OR CRY?"

Traveling by different inner clocks

Carlos Fuentes, the Mexican writer and diplomat, was once traveling in Central Mexico looking for a certain village. He stopped to ask a *campesino* how far it was to that village. The answer was: "If you had left at daybreak, you would be there now."[1]

The *campesino* had a different inner clock from those who ask questions that want an answer in miles or hours. "If you had left at daybreak, you would be there now" says that for him, travel is not just distance or time, it is a relationship of nature's rhythms, like daybreak.

This story has an important connection to the issues and questions to be raised in the essays that follow. Let me express it this way: each human being is traveling in a life. Those who read this book are among the small minority on this planet who live their lives immersed in advancing technology: computers, floppy disks, laser light disc players, digital TV sets, artificial hearts, test tube fertilization, robot farming, holography, etc. The world and the direction in which it should go are seen through the eyes of people immersed in technology. Whether we're talking about computerized credit cards or Star Wars weapons for space, we seek a progress that is centered upon what new technologies can bring. What we often forget is that the vast majority of persons on this planet do not live life immersed in the latest technology. These persons have a different inner clock. Thus in seeking answers about technology and values we are going to have to cope with two levels of concern: one for those of us who are immersed in technological change and another for those who are not. Said another way, we are going to explore the question "Why are we here?" As Carlos Fuentes put it: "Did we come here to laugh or cry?"

Technology as activity with direction

In the first decades after the Second World War, technology began to take center stage in the human activity of industrialized countries. Technology was seen as the golden road to the future. Human beings rocketed into space. Automobiles, television sets and washing machines flooded the market with a steady annual stream of new models. The energy locked in the atom was tapped and the future expanded with the image of energy as abundant and cheap as water. The Green Revolution promised to take care of the tables of the rich and the poor; it was to be a future without hunger. As United States Secretary of the Interior Stewart Udall proclaimed, "There were no problems, only solutions." All that was needed was the chance to spread the contents of the technological cornucopia to all corners of the globe.

Now, in the decade of the eighties, we have become aware of a painful reversal: it is as if there are no solutions, only problems. In 1962, Rachel Carson awakened the technological world to the fact that robins were dying due to the overuse of DDT.[2] And although the springing up of an international environmental movement has had much positive impact, we are still badgered by code words for disasters that do not go away: acid rain, radioactive waste, cancerous food additives, etc. It does not stop there, either. Societies have had to bear tremendous costs due to technological changes. Consider, for example, the exploitation of natural resources in poor countries; the fact must sink in that continued growth cannot depend on non-renewable resources. Nor can we permit great human injustices to co-exist with technological growth—for example, sacrificing people to low wages and exposure to industrial processes that ruin their health or kill them outright. The tragedy of Bhopal, India, where in 1984 more than two thousand people were killed and over two hundred thousand injured due to a chemical leak at a pesticide plant, stings even more deeply when one realizes that the workers there were paid poverty wages by any standard.

We must begin to face up to the question of the *sustainability* of modern technology. On one hand, we gain tremendous benefits from improved housing, transportation, clothing, communication, sanitation and disease control. On the other hand, we lose signfi-

5

cantly through environmental degradation, social injustice, resource depletion and our lack of control over such large centralized institutions as the military. The golden road upon which we embarked in the forties and fifties has turned out to be a toll road, and what makes the issue even more complex is that new technologies change the very way societies function! Automobiles, televisions and medical technologies, for example, have radically altered the ways we arrange our cities, use our leisure time and expect to be rescued from our health-defeating habits, whether the over-consumption of food or smoking.

As we face up to our problems we must come to grips with the fact that technology is not neutral. When we were on that golden road to the technological future, the basic assumption was that technology *was* neutral. We thought it could be used for good or ill and that we would be wise enough to choose the good. What we did not realize is that technology is only one part of a complex mix that includes economic, political, social and religious realities, all interacting in such a way that neutrality is not possible. Nuclear energy, for example, requires the existence of huge, costly, centralized institutions. It is not possible for a citizen to build a nuclear energy plant in a backyard or basement. Solar energy, on the other hand, could be developed with huge centralized institutions, but it can also be used in small decentralized ways. What a person needs to "solarize" his or her own home can be built in a basement. Neither nuclear nor solar technology is neutral towards the kind of society that will sustain it. Each represents very different social, political and economic choices, as well as the technological choice.

In short, we have learned that technology is a "god that limps." Yes, there are significant and far-reaching ills due to technological advance. But we also need to be reminded that "technology can be lovely." The fact is, however, there is no technological fix that can solve our problems. Technological fixes are for technological problems, not social or political ones. Technological ways can be found to improve nuclear and solar technologies, but they will not show us how to make the best social or political choices for the sustainability of the planet or its people. If we seek justice and growth in the quality of human life as well as the life of the planet, we will have to come up with a different economic and political will than we have at present. A will coupled with different technologies.

What is critical is not how to regulate technology by laws or restrictions, but rather how to change our *relationship* to technology through our values and discipleship choices. The important issue should be which technologies we choose to use and which we choose *not* to use because of what they do in terms of justice to person and planet. The technology that knows "the trees" *and* "the forest" is a technology that understands fact and spirit. . .*and thereby sees progress and justice as inseparable.*

The essays that follow describe the direction technology is taking and what impact that direction has on human values. What do we *want*? What do we *imagine*? What does it mean to love, to be faithful, to be a servant, to be a disciple of Jesus Christ, to respond as God's chosen people—*and* to have the technical means to change the world?

Values—as behavior and yearning

Which of the following are not values: honesty, war, smoking, currying favor, voting, wearing makeup, aspirin, privacy, planting trees, headlights on autos and rooms with windows? All are values! All represent choices we make. Values are how we do what we think is best. More precisely, as defined by Kurt Baier, values are "an attitude for or against an event or phenomenon, based on a belief that it benefits or penalizes some individual, group, or institution."[3] Our values are exposed by our behavior, and thus are observable and measurable.

Values are ways of seeing what we prize. I once heard a man describe a value he had been given as a gift by his wife. It was a clothespin with a red reflector attached. The man rode a bicycle to and from work—itself a value decision—and in order to enhance his safety, his wife gave him the clothespin-reflector to clip to the bottom of his suitcoat. Both the giving and the wearing of the reflector were expressions of value.

Though our values are known by our actions, they also have a seedbed in our yearnings. What we *think* we would like to become can be a powerful stimulus for action if we can overcome the inertia of the past. Yet how often do we see goals presented as a series of decisions that individuals and communities *can* make in order to achieve intended values? Or which can sustain their values in the presence of competing ideologies or realities? More often, we find ourselves giving in to generalizations with no sense of our power to change because we value one thing over another—as demonstrated in this conversation between a Tucson, Arizona reporter and a person on the city streets:

> "Would you like to see more industry brought to Tucson?"
> "Yes."
> "Do you think that would make our city a pleasanter place to live?"
> "No."
> "Then why do you want industry brought here?"
> "Well, you can't oppose Progress, can you?"

When we consider technological change it is crucial to know who the "controllers" are and what values they hold. For example, the values—the behavior—of the affluent often demand access to the resources of the poorer countries, but do not allow for the reverse. They are values of economic control and greed rather than of sharing and sufficiency. Richard Shaull, in *Heralds of a New Reformation: The Poor of South and North America,* wrote:

> We insist on the freedom for multinational corporations to exploit the human and material resources of poor countries and thus seem willing to go to almost any length to stop independent economic development outside that system of exploitation. We talk about freedom and democracy, and yet we support the most unjust and repressive regimes as long as they fit into our international economic schemes.[4]

In looking at our behavior in terms of our technological choices we must not avoid the matter of whose values are at stake when a particular technology is chosen. Values are not just labels for good or bad actions. They are, in an important sense, a power, an activity of the mind that can enrich or degrade living. As poetry does with words, our values make life more than a series of isolated actions. Values are activity that can hold life together or rend it asunder.

Tension—as balance between living and dying

With regard to nuclear missiles, the historian Barbara Tuchman asked: "Why do we invest all our skills and resources in a contest for armed superiority which can never be attained for long enough to make it worth having, rather than in an effort to find a modus vivendi with our antagonist—that is to say, a way of living, not dying?"[5]

Indeed, that is the nuclear tension: between living and dying, between Armageddon and future. Which do we value most? There is an important tension between living and dying with regard to choosing technologies that enhance human dignity, reverence for life and—in straightforward biblical language—peace with justice. We must also ask the question: What role does religious consciousness play if "progress" is defined in terms of technology? As Paul Davies wrote in *God and the New Physics:*

> More relevant to the decline of religion is the fact that science, through technology, has altered our lives so radically that the traditional religions may appear to lack the immediacy necessary to provide any real assistance in coping with contemporary personal and social problems. If the Church is largely ignored today it is not because science has finally won its age-old battle with religion, but because it has so radically reoriented our society that the Biblical perspective of the world now seems largely irrelevant. As one television cynic recently remarked, few of our neighbors possess an ox or an ass for us to covet.[6]

Tension always exists between what we could do and what we do. If, for example, we could divert just eight hours of global military spending ($680 million), we might be able to eradicate malaria. Since some two hundred million persons on the planet suffer from this debilitating disease, we can wonder why such a trade-off would not be possible. The point is, how does our sense of faithfulness, inspired by religious consciousness, make it possible for us to make different choices? Tension is a matter of balance. However as an Eastern saying goes, "there is more to balance than not falling over."

Nothing new, as yet

Actually, there is nothing new before us. At least nothing new in the images and concerns of the past few decades of accelerated change. The words of Ken Cauthen, from his book *The Ethics of Enjoyment* (1975), are still appropriate today:

> Thousands are dying of starvation in Asia and Africa. Inflation and recession deal a double blow at home. Prices rise and unemployment increases. In order to feed, clothe, and house a growing world population, economic growth must speed up. But increasing production pollutes the air, the land, and the sea. It also runs the

risk of using up certain nonrenewable natural resources. . . .The industrial world tells the poor countries to reduce their birthrates, since overpopulation is so dangerous. They reply that the rich nations must reduce their extravagant consumption and share their bounty with the rest of the world.[7]

After more than ten years we have still not chosen a different direction. We continue to bank on new technology to solve old technological problems. We still count on the benefits of technology trickling downward to the masses. We still face the problems of hunger, overpopulation and pollution, not to mention the kind of psychic hypnosis that hopes a "better world" will come if only we work harder and make more "progress." What has been pushed aside are dreams of quality. We are still ignoring the message in one stanza in a Stephen Geyer song recorded by John Denver: "Times are hard/ The old backyard is covered in cement/ The people seem afraid to dream/ And dreams don't cost a cent."[8]

We regret and bemoan many aspects of modern life but seem determined to stay the course and trust the illusion that some "future technological magic" will win the day. And by our choices we continue to sacrifice people and quality to the inertia of material progress. As Ivan Illich wrote:

> Plastic buckets from São Paulo are lighter and cheaper than those made of scrap by the local tinsmith in Western Brazil. But first cheap plastic puts the tinsmith out of existence, and then the fumes of plastic leave a special trace on the environment — a new kind of ghost.[9]

"If we do not change our direction," an ancient Chinese proverb says, "we are likely to end up where we are headed." As I see it, many of our present technological choices are heading us toward disaster: nuclear weapons, acid rain and the exploitation of the poor as industrialized nations rapidly consume the earth's most readily-accessible raw materials, whether oil or whales. It is not a matter of changing direction and doing away with technology; it is a matter of choosing a different technological direction. Author Robert Pirsig saw it as a matter of fusion:

> The way to solve the conflict between human values and technological needs is not to run away from technology. That's impossible. The way to resolve the conflict is to break down the barriers of dualistic thought that prevent a real understanding of what tech-

nology is—not an exploitation of nature but a fusion of nature and the human spirit into a new kind of creation that transcends both.[10]

Or as described in a colorful, but profound image in a Japanese instruction manual: "Assembly of Japanese bicycle require great peace of mind."[11]

The shape of yearning

In our tryst with technologically-defined progress, we have pushed aside our visions, our lives' inner yearnings. Strange ideas are always afoot in our world. Some claim—on scientific grounds—that death does not exist (it is only a transition) and that paranormal occurrences are not fake. Some propose that with our new space tools we should leave the earth and go out as spores into the universe. Others advise staying home and with Project Cyclops, communicate electronically with intelligent life beyond the planet. Some want to tow icebergs to the rain-thirsty deserts; others want to build mile-high buildings to house cities so that the land can be returned to its normal state. These ideas may be strange, but they are possible.

But what about strange ideas that seem impossible? What is it we yearn for? What is still on the human agenda from ages past that has not yet come to be? I'm not talking about fulfilling someone's charts on growth or consumption by the year whatever. I am talking about the yearning for justice and peace, to name two. *Shalom*, in a word. I'm talking about turning away from exploitation and greed and using our immense technological abilities to benefit all humans and all the environment.

When God sent messengers to Abraham and Sarah to tell them that they would have a son, Sarah laughed. Both were very old and Sarah had stopped having her monthly periods, so what she heard did not seem possible to her. God puzzled at her laughter and asked Abraham about it, saying, "Is there anything too hard for the Lord?" We might hear such a question directed at us. We might scoff at the possibility of peace and justice. But if God is serious, can we respond with laughter?

Where is our vision? Not in a set of idle fantasies or silly speculations, but in the terms of the Psalmists, "Love and faithfulness will meet; righteousness and peace will embrace" (85:10), or "God is our shelter and strength, always ready to help in times of trouble" (46:1).

Where is the kind of vision Elrond expressed in Tolkien's *The Fellowship of the Ring?*

> This quest may be attempted by the weak with as much hope as the strong. Yet such is oft the course of such deeds that move the wheels of the world: small hands do them because they must, while the eyes of the great are elsewhere.[12]

"Small hands do them because they must." Imagine such yearning in the pursuit of peace and justice. To turn our individually collective "small" hands and minds towards the discovery of a deep yearning for another way of being in the world is to reach beyond our reason and our technology to accept also the responsibility of the heart. To know love as progress, not just a new machine.

Yes, "Did we come here to laugh or cry?" What is it that guides our choices, motivates our hopes and challenges our future? Norman Cousins, in a 1971 Saturday Review editorial on the moon expeditions, allowed that we should not require that all the problems on earth be solved before seeking challenges in space. He reminded us, however, that we are judged by the challenges we define for ourselves. He wrote of humankind:

> So far, they have attached more importance to the challenge of adventure than to the challenge of compassion, more importance to the challenge of technological grandeur than the challenge of human growth, more importance to the challenge of war than the challenge of peace, more importance to the challenge of productivity than the challenge of perspective, more importance to the challenge of the scientific intelligence than the human spirit."[13]

The tension between our technology and our values will occupy the next eight essays before we turn to ponder another Carlos Fuentes question: "Are we dying or being born?"

> the quality of God we seek outside
> is analogous to our God within
>
> — Carolyn Kleefeld

ONE

TECHNOLOGICAL PROGRESS AND RELIGIOUS CONSCIOUSNESS

> It is not possible to dig a hole
> in a different place by digging
> the same hole deeper.
>
> Edward de Bono

Do you remember looking at "hidden pictures" in children's magazines? Perhaps it was a picture of a pond with woods around it and you were asked to see how many different animals you could find. Maybe first you saw a frog, then a duck, a bird on a tree limb, a rabbit in the bushes and so on. But there were always some that were hard to find: like the snake climbing a tree trunk! None of the animals, however, was there until you saw it, and even though you might have had trouble finding them, once you did they became so obvious you wondered how you could have missed them!

This is very much like the experience of searching out new meaning. When you start out you have one picture of something. Then if you look long and hard, with purpose and imagination, you discover another picture quite different from the first. The innocent pond and woods are now populated with all kinds of animals, birds and reptiles.

So it must be with technological progress. If something is good, our belief in progress says more of it will be even better! We have shifted from being intrigued and fascinated by change to expecting, even demanding change. (Who can even remember the introduction of seamless nylons or the move from black and white to color TV?) If it doesn't get better, bigger and brighter, something must be wrong.

Change and rhythm

Our view of change has significantly influenced our experience of rhythm. "It used to be nature," Jacques Ellul wrote, "that imposed its evolutionary rhythm upon us. Now it is technology."[1] The products and methods pouring out of our technological activity are applauded more, it seems, for the change they offer than for any satisfaction or improvement they might bring about. Consider food, for example. Since World War II there have been enormous changes in the way we encounter food. Today a computerized light scans a universal code on every package. Special symbols make for a more efficient system of inventory, pricing and checking out. In short, the marketing of food has changed its rhythm from one of a personal encounter to an impersonal transaction. The change has little to do with the food. For example, compare the effort and ingenuity required to develop the computer scanning of food packages to that which goes towards the redistribution of food to relieve hunger. The computer scan mindset toward food recognizes and rewards efficiency rather than sharing. The goal is to sell food efficiently, rather than to make it available for sustaining human life. Is it possible to arrange things so that as much time, money and imagination are spent on redistributing food as on packaging and marketing it?

My point is not to suggest that we need a good whipping-post for the ills of technological progress. Yet in our rush toward change for the sake of change we often overlook the delicate and vital rhythms of our lives. We pay too little attention to the balance between efficiency and sufficiency, between novelty and sharing. We value efficiency over justice. In a phrase, our technological progress has not included enough awareness of our religious consciousness. "In a healthy culture," historian Theodore Roszak wrote, "technological progress would be simultaneously a deepening of religious consciousness."[2]

The "deepening" of technological progress, it would seem, has been a process of digging the same holes deeper. We continue to invest time, money and energy in high tech energy solutions (if not nuclear fission, then fusion) while blithely ignoring the fact that the economic costs alone are staggering. Cheap energy is a shibboleth, an old battle cry that still stirs the soul but which will rip the bottom out of every economic pocketbook. We continue to build and design new weapons systems even though the ones we have can destroy us twenty times over or more.

I want to propose two areas to explore as we examine the relationship of religious consciousness to technological progress. The first is the possibility of a new scientific worldview. The second is a review of the radical nature of our instructions from the New Testament.

The Gaia hypothesis

James E. Lovelock and Lynn Margulis, two highly respected and widely-published scientists, have in recent years turned their attention to other-than-ordinary science. Both were trained in traditional science, yet are now seeking to develop a new scientific world view regarding nature and biological intelligence. Ever since Darwin, scientists have propagated the view that life is evolutionary. Through processes of genetic mixture, changes in living matter occur in such a way that the ones most suited to survive in their particular setting are the ones that reproduce and thus determine the direction of biological success. Darwinian evolution has been seen as a process of chance. It is inappropriate to talk in terms of goals, purpose or guidance by anything other than the scientific laws of genetics.

Two ordinary scientific questions led to the development of the unorthodox Gaia* hypothesis: (1) how does the earth's atmosphere maintain itself? (2) how does life on earth maintain itself? To answer these questions, Lovelock and Margulis began by considering the earth's atmosphere as an integral, regulated and necessary part of the biosphere. They saw it as a kind of circulatory system of the biosphere put together co-operatively by living systems to carry out certain necessary control functions. In their thinking, the entire complex system of living matter, air, oceans and land surface exhibit the behavior of a single organism, a kind of living creature which they named *Gaia*, the name given by the ancient Greeks to the goddess of Earth.[3]

In shorthand form, these are some of the ideas that have resulted from the Gaia hypothesis:
1) all species of living organisms collaborate in a grand web of biological intelligence;
2) the purpose of this life network is to keep the earth fit for life;
3) life itself controls the temperature and the chemical environment of the planet in order to ensure its own survival;
*rhymes with papaya

15

4) evolution is not a blind competition of struggling organisms but a highly intelligent collaboration.

In a Gaia worldview, the concept of biological intelligence would replace the Darwinian idea of the survival of the fittest. The integrating idea would be one of biological cooperation rather than competition. To begin to see the Earth as a whole, as "one life" would be to force a redefinition of all that we do with technology. Nature would no longer be raw material to be used as our technological ambitions dictate; nature would be a full participant—the end as well as the means.

It is the nature of a scientific worldview to change as new information becomes available. If the collaboration/cooperation idea of the Gaia hypothesis were to overturn the survival/competition basis of Darwinian evolution, many of the underlying assumptions of modern technology would disappear. A cooperative technology would be quite different from one that exploits nature!

What are our instructions as a people?

It is not my intent to prescribe the kind of religious consciousness to go with technological progress. The important thing is to engage in dialogue and to share our different religious experiences. Let me illustrate what I mean through this conversation between a young woman from the Wampanoag tribe at Mashpee, Massachusetts, and a middle-aged Caucasian woman involved in the ecological design of new human settlements.

> The general subject of our conversation was the differences in the ways of our respective cultures—hers, the ancestral traditions of the Wampanoags and ours, at least in her eyes, those of an exploitative technological society. What she said to us in essence was, My people don't understand you or why you do the things you do. We don't understand why you are still trying to take more of our land. Why must you own things. Why must you always have more. Her eyes clouded for a moment as she searched for the right explanation, then she gestured to a nearby flower bed. A seed, a flower, a tree unfolds according to the instructions it has been given. We have always tried to live by ours. We don't understand yours. How you have been taught to live. What your instructions are.[4]

That is the issue, the tough question: What are our instructions, as a people, as a culture? For Christians, instructions are found in the Bible. If, however, we look for our instructions in the values, assumptions, loyalties, myths, goals, necessities and givens of the world's cultural and ideological systems, we will be greatly pressured to accept the kind of technological progress that serves *itself* instead of others. Progress will then fulfil technology's prophecy (because it can be done it will be done) as opposed to the prophecy of servanthood (progress is needed to respond to the instructions of sacrificial love).

To find out what our biblical instructions are it is tempting to make a list: the Ten Commandments, for example. As important as that can be, let us also recognize what I call the rainbow nature of the biblical record. Just as all the colors are needed to make a rainbow, so all the biblical images and parables and stories of sin and grace, reconciliation and hard hearts are needed to form the great story that guides us in the direction God calls us to take. The biblical instructions are a tapestry, a mosaic, a rainbow of blending colors—all of them are needed.

Nevertheless, we need a place to start. We need images to work from, focal points for faithfulness. One familiar and powerful one is in Matthew 25, where we are called to feed the hungry, visit the imprisoned, clothe the naked. Other reminders are Psalm 23, "The Lord is my shepherd;" Mary's song of praise in the first chapter of Luke: "My heart praises the Lord;" the promise of Isaiah 11 that the "wolf shall dwell with the lamb;" God's promise in Genesis 9 of an everlasting covenant with all living beings on earth; the Book of Ruth's story of the blessing that came to a foreigner who turned in faithfulness to God; Paul's preaching on love in I Corinthians 13: "...if I have no love, I am nothing;" and the list goes on and on.

One that I would choose to single out is Micah 6:8, concerning what the Lord requires of us: "to do justice, and to love kindness, and to walk humbly with your God" (Revised Standard Version). As we struggle to understand what is required of us as technology and values interact, what better measuring stick could we have?

Singlemindedness

Singlemindedness, whether in technology, religion, engineering, or monasticism is not sufficient for growth in human communities. People are too diverse; societies are too complex. Unless people can integrate many levels of possibility and discovery they become automatons, repeating the past, perpetuating the injustices of the *status quo*.

Technology as a way of *looking* and *doing* has often come under fire. In 1976, an engineer named Samuel C. Florman wrote a book titled *The Existential Pleasures of Engineering*. In it, he responded to criticisms of technology raised by Lewis Mumford, Charles Reich, Rene Dubos and Theodore Roszak. Florman saw each one as an anti-technological boogeyman who would have us return to a past devoid of the progress of engineering. Since I had been profoundly influenced by the four he denounced I was both defensive and curious as I encountered Florman's ideas.

Florman does not accept the view that "the source of society's problem and man's miseries [lies] in the concept of technology itself." Instead he posits the view that "at the heart of engineering lies existential joy," and that

> the experience of the engineer demonstrates that the good life — what John Dewey called the "satisfactory" as opposed to the merely "satisfying" — is achieved by immersion in the material world, by engaging in activity which is often mundane.[5]

My physical and spiritual reflexes recoil at such flagrant single-mindedness. All those thinkers I have grown to admire and respect have put before me a vision of *multimindedness* that calls for involvement with the material, the ecstatic, the sacred, the cosmic and even the immaterial. Together they form a wellspring of surprise that both refreshes and humbles the observer. My existential pain at Florman's claim for engineering arises because for so many people, he is right. And this "rightness," I believe, is what causes us so much human and earthly anomie.

I hardly know where to begin to illustrate my discomfort at engineer Florman's willingness to find the good life only in the material, machine-making activities of humankind. Picking discomfort more or less at random, I grimace at his discussion of our place in the world:

> When man considers his place in the natural world, his first reaction is one of awe. He is so small, while the mountains, valleys and oceans are so immense. He is intimidated. But at the same instant he is inspired. The grand scale of the world invites him to conceive collossal works.[6]

In other words, the world is a big place for engineers to make even bigger things. "I'm just glad that cows don't fly," is a childhood saying that comes to mind.

In writing about machines, Florman offers:

> The engineer's first instinctive feeling about the machine is likely to be a flush of pride. For all the mistakes that have been made in its use, the machine still stands as one of mankind's most notable achievements. Man is weak, and yet the machine is incredibly strong and productive.[7]

He really didn't mean that, did he? "Man is weak. . .the machine is incredibly strong and productive." The world, in Florman's eyes, consists of bridges, elevators, cranes and airplanes. Never mind poetry, plays, sports, love or. . .wait a minute: love. Yes, Florman has something to say about that, too:

> In the *Builder of Bridges*, a long-forgotten play that graced the London stage during the first decade of this century, Edward Thursfield, resident engineer, tells his boss, Sir Henry, that he does not wish to go to Rhodesia on an engineering project because he is planning to get married.
>
> Edward: I'm in love, Chief.
>
> Sir Henry: So was I, once, but I shut myself up for a week, and worked on an air-machine. Grew so excited I forgot the girl. You try.[8]

I do not know whether to cry or laugh! To be sure, engineering is important — but to make the claim for its being the only source of the good life, of strength and productivity, and of its having more existential power than love. . .Whew, that's a singlemindedness that vibrates between historical heresy and insanity!

I would be happy to forget engineer Florman except that he does represent the view of many people. Nancy Jack Todd said it well in a sentence that I imagine those like Florman would consider frivolous: "The stars are still there to remind us that we are both trivial and non-trivial."[9] To understand that kind of image requires a blending of technological and religious consciousness that is far too absent in today's world.

The prophetic responsibility of religious commitment

I believe it is correct to say that our industrialized society does not value feeding the hungry. I say this knowing of numerous effective programs and individual efforts to feed the hungry. Indeed, the number of "night shelters" for street people has greatly increased in American cities. No, what I am saying is that the overall direction of our society does not include the value of feeding the hungry. The proof? Our behavior: having excess food that is either bartered in the international arena or which becomes outdated and then is discarded. Worse, the United States government pays farmers millions upon millions *not* to grow food or produce milk. What would it be like if our society valued people being fed, not going hungry? What if, just as we educate and support police to maintain law and order, we educated and supported people to see that no one went hungry?

The same kind of reasoning applies to our health care systems. Instead of worrying over the fact that some people are not well, we have created a complex and costly hospital system that allows access only if one has money and insurance or is a charity patient. What if our society's values said we should do *all* we can to see that *all* are healthy (just as we have the societal value that everyone should have access to public education?).

Quite often in conversations we get into a situation in which one person says, "Well, I have my view and you have yours. We're both right and there is nothing we should do to resolve our differences." But when we apply the instructions of Matthew 25, that will not work. In this chapter the outcasts from Heaven ask, "When did we see the hungry, not give the thirsty a drink, not welcome the stranger, not clothe the naked, not visit the sick and the imprisoned?" Christ's answer, well known but not well practiced, is that in rejecting or turning away the "least" ones, they had turned away from Him and life. Those who turn away are sent into eternal punishment. In our technological society, where we are rewarded by obtaining and using as many material things as we can, Christ's judgement seems odd and irrelevant. Pursue the good, the material, we hear. . .do what you can in your spare time for the appropriate downtrodden. And if you cannot, God will forgive you; Jesus has atoned for your sins. In short, we are told: never mind.

There *is*, however, a difference between feeding, clothing, lifting up the least ones and *not* doing these things. There is a judgment. And when we bless technological ways that make it even more difficult for the least ones to get food when they are hungry or care when they are sick, then we are judged. If we are serious about Matthew 25 and the least ones, we must redefine progress; we must take into account matters of the spirit as well as material things. There is more to being hungry than not having food.

Perhaps the real terror of our technological world is the way it leaves us unable to face God. The question is raised in the Book of James, chapter two: what do we gain if we have faith but not works? That is, what if we are "in favor of" feeding the poor, but continue to support agricultural technologies that actually turn people away from farming — which end up paying people *not* to grow food? Imagine, as did Barbara Ward, the British economist:

> . . .we come ultimately before our Heavenly Father, and he says, "Did you feed them, and did you give them to drink, did you clothe them, did you shelter them?" and we say, "Sorry, Lord, but we did give 0.3% of our gross national product." I don't think it will be enough.[10]

It will not be enough to say that tractors were just too expensive or that farms got bigger with fewer people or that hospitalization costs rose to over a thousand dollars a day or besides, we needed another twenty billion dollars for new military technology. No, perhaps the real terror is our inability to face God, period.

Disconnected from religious consciousness or commitment, technological progress rapidly becomes a new snake oil to cure all ills. It capitulates to a single-visioned scientific mindset. It presumes that the only way of "knowing" is to reduce everything to sheer information cleansed of feeling or mystery. Theodore Roszak calls us to recognize the need for "the prophetic dimension of religious life, which is the courage by which men and women speak truth to power in order that justice may be done." We must "revitalize the prophetic responsibility of religious commitment," and

> If never once while we are here, do we recall our loyalties and obligations to the fallen and oppressed, to the wretched and imprisoned, then we forfeit our claim to speak to humanity and God dies once again, right here in these well-upholstered corridors.[11]

TWO

THE HUMAN SCALE: TECHNOLOGY AS IF PEOPLE MATTERED

There is a story about an ancient mythical king who, pondering the difficult lives of his subjects, proposed that the whole kingdom be covered with animal skins to alleviate the roughness of the earth underneath tender human feet. Before the king's plan could be carried out, one of the members of the court pointed out that the same result could be achieved if small patches of skin were bound to each foot. This story illustrates two different attitudes toward nature. In one, we adapt nature to ourselves; in the other, we adapt ourselves to nature.

And so it is with technology: how do people fit in?

Where do people fit assumptions of progress?

Today progress is fueled by two major assumptions: (1) bigger is better; (2) if there is a problem, technology will fix it. For example, the response to the massive power failure in New York City in 1977 was to develop bigger electrical generating plants and bigger computers to guide it all. In response to the question of what happens if we run out of oil pumped from the ground: never mind, we'll develop the technology to squeeze oil out of shale. When that is gone, we will have the technology of nuclear fusion and we can forget about oil altogether. What we have been slow to realize, is that the energy crisis is basically one of too much bigness and too much technology. In our rush toward "abundant" energy we have over-looked efficiency, conservation and economic/environmental costs. Because progress is so bound up in bigness and technology it is not easy to change course — to seek balance, not giantism, or solutions and applications that have only local, not global impact. Progress guided by bigness and the "technofix" mentality is a major stumbling block to justice and to a higher quality of life. We must learn to put our values in other things than we do now.

The major guiding images of our economic world have been of expanding markets, often achieved at the expense of others. To illustrate: in genetic engineering laboratories, unique new bacteria have been created that eat oil or the deadly herbicide called Agent Orange. The idea has been to release these organisms into the environment to clean up oil spills or the aftermath of the use of chemical pesticides. In 1984, some Canadian scientists who had not as yet created any such organisms were eager to get involved. As Maurice Brossard, vice president for biotechnology at the National Research Council of Canada, said:

> There will be fantastic markets in ten years for biotechnological products or processes — in pharmaceuticals, agriculture, energy, chemistry, pulp and paper, and waste treatment. If Canada does not use the new technologies, other countries will and some of our industries will cease to be competitive.[1]

Not to single out Canada, this mindset is a prime example of the kind of thinking that prevails with regard to new technologies. I would readily believe that Mr. Brossard is well aware of the potential hazards of releasing into nature created organisms that have never existed there before. But is there any doubt that such a concern takes a distant second place to the attraction of "fantastic markets"? Or to the fear that Canada may lose the ability to be competitive? Where are values that would prefer solar energy to oil? That would reject the use of Agent Orange altogether? There must be alternatives to market and competition thinking.

While Moses was on Mount Sinai talking with God, the people of Israel got impatient and began to worry about the future. They asked Aaron to make them a god to lead them. Aaron in turn asked them to produce all the gold earrings they were wearing, and in a sweep of technological grandeur he had them melted down and transformed into a golden bull-calf. The new creation was placed in front of a newly-built altar and the people were invited to a festival to honor the Lord. The festival, however, turned into such an orgy of drinking and sex that when Moses came down off the mountain and saw it, he smashed the tablets of commandments God had given him. When Moses confronted Aaron with this abominable behavior, Aaron's defense was that Moses had been gone so long they thought he would never return; Aaron had asked for gold ornaments, thrown them into the fire, and lo and behold, out had come the golden calf!

The reason for recalling this familiar story is to remind ourselves of how readily humans will put their dependence in things rather than on relationships. Too often our notion of righting what is wrong is to make some new "thing". The technological way to alleviate traffic congestion, for instance, has been to build more highways—which only leads to more cars and more congestion. We have ignored the significance of the tablets Moses was bringing, that series of brief headlines about relationship with God, family, self, others and nature. We too easily make technology into an idol, a golden way that will solve all our problems. But our problem is not how much oil we can get or how many heart-lung machines we can make or how sophisticated a computer we can invent. Our problem is our letting technology take too much control over our lives. Too often we use our technological ability in ways that massively disrupt and even threaten life. What better example could there be than our way of arming the world with nuclear missiles capable of destroying it, and all in the name of peace? A modern-day Moses would react to our missiles "monuments" and to our exploitative technologies in the same way as he did to Aaron's golden calf: by becoming furious, then returning to God's presence and asking for forgiveness.

The questions to ponder are: What are right relationships? What is right technology?

Giantism

As Kirkpatrick Sales has pointed out, "a big party is not simply an intimate dinner with more people. . .a big corporation is not simply a family firm with more employees and products, a big government is not simply a town council with more branches."[2] Using technology as we do we are irresistibly lured by giantism. Technologists talk of drilling holes a hundred miles into the earth; they talk of releasing millions of small metal pieces into the upper atmosphere to see how things work there; they talk of converting the whole state of Wisconsin into a giant antenna in order to search for submarine movement in the oceans; they deploy fifty thousand nuclear weapons and want still more. If it is bigger it must be better. So we glorify size and power and lose contact with relationships which depend not on size and power, but on *connection*. As theologian Henri Nouwen wrote in *¡Gracias!*:

> Our salvation comes from something small, tender and vulnerable, something hardly noticeable. God, who is the Creator of the Universe, comes to us in smallness, weakness and hiddeness. I find this a hopeful message. Somehow, I keep expecting loud and impressive events to convince me and others of God's saving power; but over and over again, I am reminded that spectacles, power plays and big events are the ways of the world. Our temptation is to be distracted by them and made blind to the "shoot that shall sprout from the stump."[3]

Over twenty years ago, Leopold Kohr wrote, "Wherever something is wrong, something is too big."[4] Technological *bigness* must be set aside for technological *appropriateness*. That is, technology that is significant *where* it is being used—which rules out, for example, high-tech agriculture in Two-Thirds World countries* and nuclear weapons everywhere.

Technofix

As we are painfully learning, the kinds of technological solutions we apply often make the problems worse. For example, the chemical DDT is supposed to kill the mosquito that carries malaria. What has not been widely appreciated is the biological fact that DDT does not kill all the mosquitos. Some are "strong" enough not to die and they survive to reproduce. Soon a new population of mosquitos arises that does not succumb to DDT. So a stronger chemical is applied. Again, most mosquitos die, but not the "strong" ones. So an even stronger chemical is needed, and it turns out that this chemical is hazardous to humans. So we are in a Catch-22 dilemma: death by malaria or by chemical poisoning. What is not widely known is

---

*I use the phrase "Two-Thirds World countries" instead of the usual "Third World" as a way of reminding us that two-thirds of the people on this planet live in situations of poverty and powerlessness.

that there are *non-chemical* ways to eradicate malaria—basically, by improving the diet and general health of an affected population. California, for example, was free of malaria by 1930 through improvements in social and economic conditions. DDT was not available until the 1940's.

Another example: in the 1960's, when phosphates in detergents came under fire for causing water pollution, a widely advocated "solution" was to replace phosphate with another chemical, NTA. But the issue is not which chemical to use. If hundreds of tons of anything are added to our water systems, somewhere, somehow, at some cost we are going to have to remove them. Substituting NTA for phosphates was not a solution, it was the continuation of a problem.

The absurdity of technofix answers is aptly illustrated by a conversation between psychiatrist R. D. Laing's wife, Jutta, and their eight year old son, Adam. Jutta says in a teasing tone, "I'm going away." Adam responds, laughing, "You can't do that because I love you and if you go away I'll kill you."[5]

Another important illustration is in the area of hunger. Quoting again from Kirkpatrick Sale:

> Let's say that America wants to alleviate the crisis of domestic hunger, not simply for humanitarian reasons but because feeding 20 million underfed citizens turns them into better workers, better consumers, and better taxpayers and prevents them from turning to social unrest. But given the nature of corporate agriculture, a decision to grow more food means a far greater use of energy for farm equipment, fertilizers, pesticides, and transportation to markets, thus adding to the energy crisis, driving up energy prices, and making the price of growing and distributing food even more expensive, thus ultimately putting it out of the price-range of the needy. It means increased use of pesticides, some of which in the air, soil, or food will cause additional disease and debilitation, especially among the poor, thus putting them out of work and limiting the amount of money they can spend on food. It means the expansion of the larger farms with greater capital, thus driving out small and marginal farmers who will be forced into the cities and either join the ranks of the underfed or get on the welfare rolls, adding to governmental spending and thus to inflation, driving up food prices. With increased inflation and abundant agricultural supplies, farmers will be getting less money for their crops, so either they will have to be given subsidies from the Federal treasury, in-

creasing inflation still further, particularly for the poor, or they will have to cut back on production to force prices up, thus making less food available for the underfed.[6]

The technofix approach all too often ignores its impact on the poor. E. F. Schumacher put it clearly when he wrote in despair:

> We have science and technology to help us along the road to peace and plenty, and all that is needed is that we should not behave stupidly, irrationally, cutting into our own flesh. The message to the poor and discontented is that they must not impatiently upset or kill the goose that will assuredly, in due course, lay golden eggs also for them. And the message to the rich is that they must be intelligent enough from time to time to help the poor, because this is the way by which they will become richer still.[7]

The "what is best for the rich must be best for the poor" strategy ignores the poor because technological development is geared toward power, not sharing. Schumacher is again right on target when he laments the nature of the aid given to the poor and the kind of technology imposed on them:

> The aid-givers—rich, educated, town based—know how to do things in their own way; but do they know how to assist self-help among two million villages, among two thousand million villagers—poor, uneducated, country-based? They know how to do a few big things in big towns; but do they know how to do thousands of small things in rural areas? They know how to do things with lots of capital; but do they know how to do them with lots of labour—initially untrained labour at that?[8]

Gandhi drew attention to the same matter when he commented on the problem with machines: "Every machine that helps every individual has a place, but there should be no place for machines that concentrate power in a few hands and turn the masses into machine-minders, if indeed they do not make them unemployed."[9]

Prolonging life or dying?

Let me illustrate the matter of the human scale and technofix in quite a different way, by pointing to the dilemma of dying in a technological society. It is well known that medical technology has developed sophisticated and powerful machines that can keep a person alive far beyond the occurrence of what used to be a "cause of death." This technology has presented us with complex questions of both economics and values. How much can society afford to spend on the terminally ill? Colorado Governor Richard D. Lamm, in a 1984 political campaign, raised this issue in a most candid way. He began with the obvious observation that we all will die. Then he made a value judgment: it is wrong to prolong a life beyond reasonable limits. In talking about one's "duty to die," Lamm explained:

> It's like if leaves fall off a tree, forming the humus for other plants to grow out [of]. We've got a duty to die and get out of the way with all our machines and artificial hearts and everything else like that and let the other society, our kids, build a reasonable life.[10]

Yes, and what are the reasonable limits? How are we going to determine how many artificial hearts become available? Are we going to ask society to pay five hundred or a thousand dollars a day to keep each one of an increasing number of terminally ill persons alive for an indefinite period? Are these machines actually prolonging life or prolonging dying?

As James M. Wall observed in an editorial in *The Christian Century*, Governor Lamm not only dared to challenge the medical science practitioners on what they were doing, but on *why* they were doing it. Wall suggested that we have replaced "the religious dogma that God is to be trusted. . .with scientific dogma that everything that can be done must be done." And further: "The dogmas of technolatry must be examined with the same unblinking scrutiny that science gave medieval religious dogmas.[11]

Technology on a human scale means that just because we *can* do something to prolong life, that is not sufficient justification for actually doing it. We must also be aware of how we use our limited resources: which special interest groups are demanding their slice of the pie at the expense of the general public? There is no simple answer. But a new joining of technological prowess with religious commitment is crucial.

Centralization

Some of the technology we impose on ourselves requires massive centralization, which in turn can lead to widespread disaster. Farmer and poet Wendell Berry has described the 1975 Michigan farm disaster when "a fire-retarding chemical known as PBB was mistaken for a trace mineral and mixed into a large order of live-stock feed." The contaminated feed was widely distributed and before it could be withdrawn, it destroyed "about 1.5 million chickens, 29,000 head of cattle, 5,920 hogs, 1,470 sheep, 2,600 lb. of butter, 18,000 lb. of cheese, 34,000 lb. of dry milk products, and 5 million eggs."[12] There is tragedy enough in this destruction, not to mention unknown long-term effects on human health. But Berry was getting at another kind of disaster when he wrote that:

> this tragedy is characteristic of an agriculture, indeed of a culture, without margins. In a highly centralized and industrialized food-supply system there can be no small disaster. Whether it be a production 'error' or a corn blight, the disaster is not foreseen until it exists; it is not recognized until it is widespread. By contrast, a highly diversified, small-farm agriculture combined with local marketing is literally crisscrossed with margins, and these margins work both to allow and encourage care and to contain damage.[13]

In our enchantment with technological changes in agriculture based on chemical fertilizers and pesticides we have put aside not only centuries of human agricultural wisdom, but have put aside nature's wisdom in terms of its diversity. Our technological triumph over agriculture is based on an assumption that might can win out. This completely ignores a basic fact of creation: nature's ability to heal and organize itself through diversity.

Seen from the perspective of the world's poor, the industrialized countries have made a powerful value choice. This choice comes through clearly in the dynamics of global agricultural systems. Much has been written about the Green Revolution in terms of improved seeds and better fertilizers. What gets much less attention is that many Two-Thirds World countries are trapped into growing export food for industrialized countries in order to earn foreign currency to use in international markets. The peasant farmers in Mexico who grow strawberries and tomatoes, or in Senegal, who grow ground-nuts and vegetables for export do not produce rice or beans for the use of their own communities and families. Many Two-Thirds World countries have huge agricultural sectors devoted to procuring cash for large landowners—not for feeding local people.

The Green Revolution has certainly achieved many remarkable breakthroughs. Not as widely discussed, however, are two related factors: population and social success. With regard to population, it is projected that two billion people will be added to the globe by the year 2000. In other words, the population is expected to increase by over two hundred thousand persons a day between now and 2000 A.D. While the Green Revolution is credited as being the major factor in doubling the global supply of food between 1950 and 1980, the question is: can it achieve that same rate of growth in the face of this continuing increase in population? Equally important is the matter of social success: justice. To illustrate how these two factors are interrelated, let us consider an example from Malaysia.

In Northern Malaysia a ninety-million dollar dam was built in the 1960's that allowed for increased irrigation, which in turn enabled farmers to produce two crops of high-yield rice per year instead of one. By the middle 1970's, rice output had tripled. Malaysia had moved from 30 percent to 90 percent self-sufficiency in rice. Wealthier farmers increased their average incomes by 150 percent and poorer farmers by 50 percent. Thus although both richer and poorer farmers advanced, the gap between them increased. In the middle 1970's, however, rice yields leveled off as maximum growth rates were achieved. Even applying more fertilizer did not increase production. As a result, real income for both groups of farmers began to drop and by 1979, the poorer farmers were back to pre-Green Revolution levels. The richer farmers, on the other hand, attempted to avoid income reductions by buying up land from the poorer farmers. This in turn meant that the poorer farmers either became their tenants or left the land altogether. The bottom line has been a widening of the gap between the well-to-do and the impoverished, as well as a leveling-off in food production (still in the face of increasing population). The only two countries of the Green Revolution to avoid this pattern have been China and Sri Lanka.[14]

Frequently we hear that American food is helping the world's poor, that it is only because of America's tremendous agricultural proficiency that millions are kept alive. If that were true, where is the reduction in world hunger? Why is there less and less farmland in use in the United States? Why are some American farmers paid *not* to produce food?

As it turns out, the American demand for imported food, coupled with a demand for high-tech agricultural methods both at home and in other countries, has worsened the global hunger situation. The Green Revolution has favored those largest and richest Two-Thirds World farmers who can afford expensive First World technologies. Alternatively, appropriate technology can solve a country's hunger problem. The difficulty, of course, is that the political and economic values of power far outweigh the values required to provide food for everyone.

Shift toward soft technology

The alternative open to us is technology on a *human* scale.[15] There is considerable evidence that smaller communities, farms, factories and economic networks are both more efficient and more humane than larger ones. They operate with technologies that bring things back to a human scale. This would mean for example, running a centralized institution with smaller, more controllable, more efficient people-sized units which would be rooted in local circumstances and guided by local citizens. The irony for us in the developed world is that this sounds very much like what happens in a village, something to which, in our rush towards bigness, we have turned up our noses. The truth of the matter is that the history of humankind is a history of villages. The advent of cities of over a million is only a few centuries old. And only in this century have we developed megapolises of ten to twenty million people. By the year 2000, fifty-seven cities are expected to have a population of over five million, forty-two of these cities in the Two-Thirds World. In our rush to technologically-based giantism we have spurned a wisdom many centuries old.

Technology on a human scale, with a human face, would be a shift toward what has been called alternative, intermediate or "soft" technology. Science writer Robin Clarke has prepared a chart (see page 32) that compares the different characteristics of decentralized, nature-integrating, quality-valuing *soft* technology with centralized, nature-alienating, quantity-valuing *hard* technology. Reflecting on these contrasts shows that there is a significant choice at stake.[16]

The essence of soft technology is the attempt to find the appropriate balance between technologies that evolved through tradition (say, a hand hoe) and sophisticated, expensive technologies (say, a combine harvester so costly it would bankrupt a small farmer). Soft technology values balance and harmony for individuals and communities. Its impact, as John V. Taylor expressed it, has "the immediate effect of enlarging rather than diminishing the human beings whose strength and skill it augments."[17]

Said another way, we must bring a new *attitude* to our technology.

	HARD TECHNOLOGY	SOFT TECHNOLOGY
1.	Ecologically unsound	Ecologically sound
2.	Large energy input	Small energy input
3.	High pollution rate	Low or no pollution rate
4.	"One-way" use of materials and energy sources	Reversible materials and renewable energy sources only
5.	Mass production	Craft industry
6.	High specialization	Low specialization
7.	Nuclear family, city emphasis	Communal units, village emphasis
8.	Alienation from nature	Integrating with nature
9.	World-wide trade	Local bartering
10.	Innovation regulated by profit and war	Innovation regulated by need
11.	Growth-oriented economy	Steady-state economy
12.	Capital intensive	Labour intensive
13.	Alienates young and old	Integrates young and old
14.	Operating modes too complicated for general comprehension	Operating modes understandable by all
15.	Agricultural emphasis on monoculture	Agricultural emphasis on diversity
16.	Quantity criteria highly valued	Quality criteria highly valued
17.	Food production specialized industry	Food production shared by all
18.	Work undertaken primarily for income	Work undertaken primarily for satisfaction
19.	Strong work/leisure distinction	Weak or non-existent work/leisure distinction
20.	High unemployment	(concept not valid)
21.	Science and technology performed by specialist elites	Science and technology performed by all
22.	Science and technology divorced from other forms of knowledge	Science and technology integrated with other forms of knowledge

To illustrate, Wendell Berry has contrasted two character types: the exploiter and the nurturer. (See page 33).[18]

Whether considering a chart of hard versus soft technology or the contrast between the exploiter and the nurturer, it becomes clear that if we consider the human scale when we make a technological choice we will have to embrace different values. Choosing to share,

	FOR THE EXPLOITER	FOR THE NURTURER
the standard is:	efficiency	care
the goal is:	money & profit, mine before yours	health for land, self, family, community
the effort is:	to earn as much as possible with as little effort as possible	to work as well as possible
the thinking is:	numbers, quantity, hard facts	character, quality condition, kind
the activity is:	one of selling	one of craft

to recycle, to repair instead of replace, to depend on local ingenuity instead of outside expertise, to develop local products instead of depending on imported ones — each of these is a value choice that would require different technologies than the ones we employ now. Such a transition would certainly take time and a reordering of expectations and needs. Perhaps the first place to begin would be to do without what is not needed: extravagant packaging, food additives, junk mail and bombs.

The yellow brick road to the Emerald City

It helps to remember that we have gotten where we are now in the span of a few decades through massive changes in our values and technology. Particularly when we accept the fact that the road we are now on is fraught with crises and deterioration in the quality of life, we must believe that it is possible to change directions again. Maybe one way to put it is in the terms of the conversation between Dorothy and the Wizard of Oz: "You are a very bad man," Dorothy told the Wizard. "No, my dear, I'm a very good man," the Wizard replied, "I'm just a very bad wizard." The scale and direction of our technology are making things worse; yes, even for the rich who find themselves increasingly less secure and alienated. And certainly things are getting worse for the poor. We are not yet good wizards.

At the end of the yellow brick road lies the Emerald City and the Wizard of Oz, who behind his curtain makes everything in the city work. It is an idyllic city except for one thing: the Wicked Witch of the West. In one sense we are like Dorothy, the Scarecrow, the Lion and the Tinman—all standing in front of the high altar of technology to ask "it" for gifts. But unlike those four, we are not trembling in fright; rather, we are somewhat piqued. We demand that "it" produce and cut all the crap about pollution. We believe that technology can save itself, that the highest calling of technologists is to solve the problems they themselves create. And we give them the money to do it.

But there are some, like Toto, who wonder where all the noise is coming from, who in their wandering about have pulled the curtain back and are now asking if all those buttons and dials and levers are what we really want. Maybe Kansas is better than a green-domed city. Maybe we can even find a way to live with the old witch instead of doing her in. Maybe we should promote a heresy—like voluntary simplicity, organic food growing, indoor composting of human waste, peanut butter from peanuts only, making gifts instead of buying them, wood stoves, windmills, arks, neighborhoods, bartering, quilting bees and sweat equity instead of bank loans. . .as if to say with our lives, rather than with promises, "Thank you very much, Mr. Wizard, for the show, but I think I'll walk to Kansas. After all, the flowers along the road are prettier when seen from the road than from the air."

Technology as if people mattered would embrace wisdom and understand the need for justice and faithfulness. It would be technology that contributes to the fulfillment of Mary's song of praise— filling of the hungry with good things and sending away the mighty and the rich with empty hands. It would be a technology that springs, as E. F. Schumacher wrote, from a new orientation and wisdom:

> Ever bigger machines, entailing ever bigger concentrations of economic power and exerting ever greater violence against the environment, do not represent progress: they are a denial of wisdom. Wisdom demands a new orientation of science and technology towards the organic, the gentle, the non-violent, the elegant and beautiful.[19]

If you want to have deep
experiences, put yourself where
they can happen.

— anonymous

THREE

WHATEVER HAPPENED TO MYSTERY?

i have a friend. . .
who shows me the black between the stars.

—Gale Rhodes

Wizened magic-man
Catches sadness in gnarled hands,
Crumbles it to a fine frozen powder
And, tossing it into a dark sky,
Makes stars.

—Don Esty

We have always looked into the sky and beyond. And we have names for everything we can see; the Big Dipper, Venus, CX-1047, red giants and white dwarfs, Alpha Centuari. Even for what we cannot see: black holes and infinity. As humans we search and label and expand our awareness of what surrounds us, whether in millions of light years or in millionths of microns.

Names, labels and how things work

Names are only clues. We can label stars and planets and devise grand logical theories of how we have come to be and what the next billion years will do to our nook of the universe. But is that

35

where the "satisfaction" comes from when we look to the night sky, rattling off names until memory fails us and books are consulted? No, looking at the stars can be an experience of receiving, of being looked-at by something nameable. . .not a spirit or goblin, but something unlabelable. There is more to the night sky than names. Do you know a person when you know just his or her name?

How do we experience the world? Engineer Samuel Florman, in referring to the book *How Things Work*, wrote as if knowledge were only labels:

> It contains straightforward discussions of electricity and magnetism, internal combustion engines and rockets. With the help of simple diagrams, it explains the workings of carburetors, thermostats, transistors and dozens of other devices. Where is all the mystery?

Yes, engineer, where is all the mystery? What is there besides a rational explanation? Is mystery the gap between what we know and don't know? "What if I fell in the forest? Would a tree hear?" asks Annie Dillard.

To know how things work is to know only the labels for pieces, places and events. To know the night sky is to experience, along with Rhodes and Esty (quoted at the beginning of essay), the space between the labels and the magic of the toss, not its odds.

Why an essay on mystery in a book about technology? Is it not the aim of science and technology to push the frontiers of knowledge back so that we know more and more? Yes. But that is not all. And so here is an essay on mystery. If the purpose or reason for knowing is only to "explain something," then a significant aspect of knowing is lost. To be sure, there are times when expert knowledge is necessary; for example, flying a 747 jet or building a bridge. Just as surely, there are times when the presence of mystery is necessary; for example, falling in love — or experiencing communion. One might say, though, wait a minute! Flying a 747 requires technology; falling in love does not. Agreed. But therein lies the need for mystery. In our current world view, scientific and technological information has so much power that what is seen as guiding importance is objective, quantifiable description. But there is another world view, the one we encounter in Psalm 139: 13-15, as the Psalmist entreats God:

You created every part of me;
you put me together in my
mother's womb.
I praise you because you are to
be feared;
all you do is strange and
wonderful.
I know it with all my heart.
When my bones were being
formed,
carefully put together in my
mother's womb,
when I was growing there in
secret,
you knew that I was there—
you saw me before I was born.

To seriously encounter the Psalmist's words is quite a different matter than to accept the objective facts of human birth. As we try to understand what we think about abortion or euthanasia it is equally important to probe the Psalmist's words as it is to hear scientific experts testify as to the quantifiable facts about birth and death. To wonder is as important as to know.

Where is mystery? All around us, if we would look and let ourselves be seen. In our world, mystery has been degraded by continual explanation of how things work. But experience is richer for knowing the stars and the black between them. Mystery is a necessary ingredient for filling the cup of life to overflowing. Without mystery there is a hole in the cup and no amount of facts will restore it to wholeness.

At the Earlham College 1984 commencement a graduate began her remarks with a plea for recognizing that although the seniors had completed a curriculum designed to impart knowledge to them, there were deeper secrets and callings from life. She said: "There is a life force pulsing through us that insists there is another way to be. At one time or another each of us has known this to be true."

We act as if our ultimate success depends only on discovering all the laws of nature; we treat them like a piano keyboard—our task is to find all the keys. But there is more to music than striking keys and making sounds.

I want to suggest that there are ways we can explore the idea of mystery and broaden our notions of success, the good life and progress to include ways of knowing other than scientific. In the Western world, spirit and matter have been separated from each other. Prime importance has been given to matter; secondary, even trivial importance has been given to the spirit. And that flies directly in the face of biblical wisdom. Consider, for example, the reality of prayer. At Gethsemane, when confronted by deep inner sorrow, struggling to know God's will, Jesus turned his body and soul over to prayer. Who would attempt to explain how that praying worked for Jesus? Its power was in the mystery of letting go so that God could fill. To expect science or technology to devise a mechanism for explaining prayer is to take the position that "everything" is understandable. But in this instance, understanding is not the point. The power of prayer lies in answers that come when we finally let go of our need for answers and our need for being in control. Prayer is related to mystery in a way that technological thinking can never approach.

To search the realm of mystery one has to be open to a multitude of puzzles, none of which will be "solved" by scientific logic. One has to wrestle with the Zen phrase: "The instant you speak about a thing, you miss the mark." Or to use another Zen image: "What is the sound of one hand clapping?"

The great slow gestures of trees

There is great power and mystery in experiencing nature on its own terms. Ursula K. LeGuin, in *A Wizard of Earthsea,* wrote about Ged, the searcher:

> From that time on he believed that the wise man is one who never sets himself apart from other living things, whether they have speech or not, and in later years he strove long to learn what can be learned, in silence, from the eyes of animals, the flight of birds, the great slow gestures of trees.[2]

Yes, "the great slow gestures of trees." Our modern time scales tend toward the instantaneous: light at the flick of a switch, supper at the punch of a microwave dial, instant TV replay of a football play. I am not suggesting that everyone should buy a bird book and pair of binoculars, though watching the "flight of birds" is certainly a rewarding experience. I am talking, rather, about a change in mindset. A change toward nature. A shift away from seeing nature as only a source of raw materials for the engines of technology. This change in attitude and action seeks to learn significant things from the natural world on its own terms. "It used to be nature that imposed its evolutionary rhythm upon us. Now it is technology. . ." is the way theologian Jacques Ellul expressed it.[3] The changes required of us are spiritual. Finding meaning in "the great slow gestures of trees" is a habit of mind we must require of both poets and technologists. Both must take seriously such an image if we are to reap justice from our actions.

The Tao of physics

"When the only tool you have is a hammer," psychologist Abraham Maslow wrote, "everything begins to look like a nail." And so it has been with physics. When the only tool it has is mathematics, everything begins to look like a number. The world is reduced to logic and objectivity. The simpler and more comprehensive the statement, the better. Except it has not turned out that way. In the time of Newton, physicists began to work out the mathematical principles of the laws of motion. They did a superb job. Nature, they explained, was like a machine. Given enough time and effort, its clockwork could be worked out to define not only the present, but also the past and the future. Physicists later discovered, however, that as elegant and powerful as these laws might be, they did not apply when the speed considered was close to that of light — or if the object in question was an atom. When they entered these two realms, physicists discovered that physics was not just a matter of inventing new tools; for tools, in the usual sense, would not work. In a word, physicists were beginning to encounter the world of mystics.

Fritjof Capra's superbly written and mind-challenging book *The Tao of Physics* is based on the idea that "the concepts of modern physics often show surprising parallels to the ideas expressed in the religious philosophies of the Far East," (e.g., of Hinduism, Buddhism and Taoism).[4] Capra points out that the birth of modern science occurred in the fifteenth century when empirical (experimental) knowledge was combined with mathematics. Then in the seventeenth century, under the influence of Descartes, nature was divided into two separate and independent realms. One was mind and the other matter. Thus the development of modern science sprang from a worldview that saw the material world as dead and separate from life—nothing but a "multitude of different objects assembled into a huge machine."

In his wide-ranging review of Eastern mysticism and modern physics Capra concluded that "Eastern mysticism is based on direct insights into the nature of reality and physics is based on the observation of natural phenomena in scientific experiments."[5] Both mystical experiences and physics experiments require years of training under experienced masters. Both are highly sophisticated and inaccessible to the layperson. "The complexity and efficiency of the physicist's technical apparatus is matched, if not surpassed, by that of the mystic's consciousness—both physical and spiritual—in deep meditation."[6]

But the crucial comparison is similarity:

> In modern physics, the universe is thus experienced as a dynamic, inseparable whole which always includes the observer in an essential way. In this experience, the traditional concepts of space and time of isolated objects, and of cause and effect, lose their meaning. Such an experience, however, is very similar to that of the Eastern mystics.[7]

There are parallels between the different worldviews developed by physicists and by mystics. One is the recognition that to "split" our experience of existence into two camps, the spiritual and the material, may lead to a destructive one-sidedness, an excess of spirit or of matter. The complementarity is essential. But alas, it is too often lost through our faith in technological solutions.

With regard to mystery, Capra put it this way:

> In trying to understand the mystery of Life, man has followed many different approaches. Among them, there are the ways of the scientist and mystic, but there are many more: the ways of poets, children, clowns, shamans, to name but a few. These ways have resulted in different descriptions of the world, both verbal and nonverbal, which emphasize different aspects. All are valid and useful in the context in which they arose. All of them, however, are only descriptions, or representations, of a reality and are therefore limited. None can give a complete picture of the world.[8]

To be whole persons we need physical and spiritual consciousness, observation and insight, experiment and meditation, technology and mystery.

A new relationship, not information

Luke 24 reports the familiar "road to Emmaus" story about two men who were walking from Jerusalem to Emmaus when they were joined by the resurrected Jesus, whom they did not recognize. The men told their unknown walking companion the amazing events of the past few days, from the crucifixion to the women's reports of the empty tomb. When they got to Emmaus they had a meal together and in that act of sharing bread, their eyes were opened and they recognized Jesus. In their excitement to share the news they walked right back to Jerusalem to find the disciples.

Most often, this story is told to help us ponder the miracle of the risen Christ, how he appeared to men and women to demonstrate the power of the resurrection and to fulfil the scriptures. Jesus was the redeemer of Israel, who showed by his life, by his death and now by his resurrection that people could set out on a new path of reconciliation, of compassion, of justice and of love expressed in serving others. But theologian Robert McAfee Brown points out that there is another significance to the men learning the identity of the stranger:

> Only when they break bread together, when they move from words to deeds does clarity come. He was not known to them in the discussions on the road, Luke reports, 'he was known to them in the breaking of the bread' (Luke 24:35). What they now receive through Jesus' action is not more information but a new relationship.[9]

A new relationship. That was the significance of Jesus' appearance. There was no need for more words, more information. The post-resurrection need was for a new relationship. And if we truly are to seek reconciliation, compassion, justice and a sharing love, we must also connect our technological information to the relationship we desire. We cannot keep them separate. If we pursue or use technological information without paying attention to how it affects relationships, we are breaking our relationship with God. It is unjust to continue to produce hazardous nuclear wastes, for instance, when we do not know how to store them safely. It is unjust to build a dam on a Philippines river to produce electricity for Manila and at the same time wipe out a centuries-old settlement of indigenous peoples.

If we "walk" along simply sharing information (technology) without also considering its relationship to reconciliation and love, then we break our relationship with the resurrected Christ who revealed himself in the act of "breaking bread together." By pointing to the Emmaus passage I am not saying that it will somehow instruct us about what kind of technology to use. I am saying that if we take Jesus seriously, as we also should our technology, how we then decide which technology to use depends on what we intend to do about our relationships of reconciliation, compassion, justice and love. *Shalom* must be accounted for in the overall picture. Theologian John V. Taylor has defined shalom as "the harmony of a caring community informed at every point by its awareness of God."[10] *Shalom* requires our willingness to participate in the inescapable mystery of a relationship with God. The wholeness, the *shalom* comes out of the experience of that mystery, not out of a set of rules.

The choice is not between technology and no technology; it is a matter of which kind of technology. There are huge differences, for example, between the technology involved in fertilizer/pesticide/giant monocrop agriculture and that involved in compost/crop-rotation/small multicrop agriculture. The former mainly serves the needs of technological sophistication, whereas the latter, based on natural rhythms, centers on feeding people a basic, balanced diet. Equally, there is a huge difference between building bigger storehouses and losing one's life in order to gain it, as Jesus challenged us to do.

The dilemma of waiting

Physician and writer Lewis Thomas, in an essay on altruism, declared his belief that all humans, regardless of race or geographic origin, are close enough to their genetic make-up

> to warrant a biological mandate for all of us to do whatever we can to keep the rest of us, the species, alive. I maintain, despite the moment's evidence against the claim, that we are born and grow up with a fondness for each other, and we have genes for that.[11]

Then he declares the dilemma, wherein lies our challenge:

> We can be talked out of it, for the genetic message is like a distant music and some of us are hard-of-hearing. Societies are noisy

affairs, drowning out the sound of ourselves and our connection. Hard-of-hearing, we go to war. Stone-deaf we make thermonuclear missiles. Nonetheless, the music is there, waiting for more listeners.[12]

And so is mystery waiting.

Loren Eiseley, anthropologist and poetic explorer of mystery, was in the habit every autumn of searching again hopefully for the secret of life. He wrote in *The Immense Journey:* "On some day when the leaves are red, or fallen, and just after the birds are gone, I put on my hat and old jacket, and over the protests of my wife that I will catch cold, I start my search."[13] The search would begin with a "climb, instead of jump" over a wall and then into the unkempt fields and woods. Eiseley would look at it all in silence, ponder the varieties of seeds and wonder how living things had emerged from some "warm little pond." He understood that there existed a mystery of life. That is why he went every autumn into its presence as a ritual of search for what he knew would never be found.

Eiseley was not an obstinate anti-technologist. He used scientific methods in his anthropological research. But he knew that for a full life it was essential to ponder the riddle of existence and to incorporate both the pondering and the riddle into his daily experience. Mystery is important *as mystery* and is not in need of explanation, as technologists are wont to believe. Thus Eiseley pondered:

> If the day comes when the slime of the laboratory for the first time crawls under man's direction, we shall have great need of humbleness. It will be difficult for us to believe, in our pride of achievement, that the secret of life has slipped through our fingers and eludes us still. We will list all the chemicals and the reactions. The men who have become gods will pose austerely before the popping flashbulbs of news photographers, and there will be few to consider—so deep is the mind-set of an age—whether the desire to link life to matter may not have blinded us to the more remarkable characteristics of both.[14]

If you are one who gives mystery its proper place, then you are one who might do as Eiseley said: "As for me, if I am still around on that day, I intend to put on my old hat and climb over the wall as usual."[15]

<u>FOUR</u>

THE NEW LITERATURE: COMPUTERS

BlooP, FlooP, and GlooP are not trolls, talking ducks or the sound made by a sinking ship—they are three computer languages, each one with its own special purpose. These languages were invented. . ." wrote Douglas Hofstadter in *Godel, Escher, Bach*.[1] And that is the computer point: the invention of languages, the creation of a new literature, the presence of new commands and images in the human community. These new languages may well be universal, like music, with only cultural variations. But can you imagine the conceptual and spiritual leap most of the world's people will have to make as computer languages spread?

The rules of the game

As computers become capable of more and more they will more and more shape our values. My concern is not to debate which computer system is best, but rather to wonder who will have control over information and whose values will be promoted; in short, whose language will prevail.

To put it another way, let us consider the rules of the game. There are military computer programs that calculate the distribution of weapons, strategic targets and relative military strengths that can be used to help policymakers decide what next moves would "minimize" the chances of "losing" the game. The point is not to blame the computer. No, wrote anthropologist Gregory Bateson, the point is that

> . . . if you do what the computer advises, you assert by that move that you support the rules of the game which you fed into the computer. You have affirmed the rules of that game.[2]

What should we do if we want to change the rules of the game of computer military programming? Or, in general terms, which values should direct the development and use of the new literature from computers?

There is no need anymore to argue that the computer revolution is coming. It is here, and the speed of its increasing influence, as well as its changing abilities, is rocket-like on both counts. Perhaps the most characteristic symbol of this revolution is the combination of a sharp drop in costs at the same time as a spectacular increase in capacity. As expressed in *Computerworld* magazine: "If the auto industry had done what the computer industry has done in the last 30 years, a Rolls-Royce would cost $2.50 and get 2,000,000 miles to the gallon."[3]

Jerry Mander, in an article titled, "Six Grave Doubts About Computers," pointed out that every technology begins with a wave of propaganda about all the marvelous things it will provide, all the problems it will solve. He wrote:

> The first several waves of news concerning a technological invention are invariably positive, even Utopian. This is so because the information comes mostly from the people who stand to gain from society taking the favorable view. In the United States, these are the corporate people and their colleagues in science. Neither has a stake in reporting any down side to the story. As a result, most people gain their early insights and understandings from an agenda provided by biased sources. Passive to the introduction of new technologies—whether cars, nuclear energy, television or, now, computers—by the time we begin to notice problems, the technologies have advanced to a point where it is difficult to do anything about them. Obviously, our protection lies in developing our own agenda of questions and answers *early* in the process.[4]

At the present stage of the rapid expansion of computers perhaps we are overdue to wonder seriously about the power of language.

Although this is not specifically related to computers, I think of the domination of male pronouns in the English language. Concerns about inclusive language raise important questions of value and meaning. The shift toward more inclusive language cannot help but enhance both femaleness and maleness and yield a quality of human relationship significantly better than its historical procedent.

I also think about the potential dangers of the "computer mentality" using computer languages or metaphors in our work as well as our play. Perhaps it would be good to reflect again on the story of the Tower of Babel. I'm not talking about the mixing up of language so that the people of Babel were unable to understand each other. Rather, my attention focuses on the comment of the Lord that "this is just the beginning of what they are going to do. Soon they will be able to do anything they want!" In other words, it was the age-old dilemma of humans playing god. As computer languages and metaphors become a greater part of our everyday lives they will inevitably reshape our view of the world. Think of the chasm that could develop between those who utilize a computer-based worldview and those who do not. Think of the new form of injustice that could arise through the arrogance of the computer-wise demanding systems and structures that fit "their" way. We have already demanded that the Two-Thirds World accept certain technologies and hardware we have created relating to energy, agriculture, health care and weapons. Now we are poised to "give" them a technology that carries with it unique language possibilities. Will they have to do it our way once again? Or is there inherent in computer technology the ability to use a multitude of languages?

The subjective computer

I want now to look at the matter of how computers are redefining our thinking about ourselves. Sherry Turkle, author of *The Second Self: Computers and the Human Spirit* referred to this phenomenon as the "subjective computer:"

> This is the machine as it enters into social life and psychological development, the computer as it affects the way that we think, especially the way we think about ourselves . . . The question is not what will the computer be like in the future, but instead, what will *we* be like?[5]

It is as one video game player said: "When I play pinball . . . I am playing with a material. When I play asteroids, it's like playing with a mind." What is the nature of this adaptation or interaction? And how is it changing what we think about ourselves? Craig Brod, in *Technostress,* wrote about a sense of self:

> Complex adaptation occurs under more drastic circumstances — for example, when children leave home to attend school for the first time. They must be able to master enough independence to meet a new authority and to come to terms with new demands on them. When they adapt to the necessities of the new situation, something happens inside them; the way they think and feel about the world changes. They experience their lives in new ways after mastering the new situation. Their sense of self is altered.[6]

Even for many of us in the industrialized world, computers have been a new, often strange technology to encounter. It is obvious that as the number of programmers and computer salespersons continues to increase, large numbers of us are making the transition. For children, the situation is quite different. Turkle summed it up in one sentence: "Growing up with a technology is a special kind of experience."[7] To children, it is not a matter of having to learn a new and different way; it is the way. The machines have even become a medium for their own self-expression.

Relationships that relate back

What happens when we relate to a machine that relates back? The technology of movies significantly altered the medium of entertainment. Watching a story on a bigger-than-life screen, we often forget it is only a two-dimensional record on film. Emotions become powerful; we cry and laugh. But the movie does not relate back; we cannot change what is happening on the screen. The director and the actors, for good or bad, tell the story. If we yearn for more it is not possible. The advent of television brought this medium of storytelling into our living rooms, though with one significant difference: breaking up the story with advertisements. Thus the emotional impact is segmented and we become disconnected from reality.

Things are quite different with the computer. Computers are not just calculators that do mathematics that humans do not have the patience to do. In one sense they are information objects. But in the use of that information the same thing happens as with language: symbols are manipulated; meaning arises. The program in the computer becomes another mind with which to interact. You learn its intentions and then follow them. If that is not what you want, you can change the program — or, in psychological terms, change the computer's "mind."

Software is what we call the set of symbols of a computer program that allows you to "use" the computer. While the computer itself is referred to as hardware, the programs are referred to as "soft". They are pliable, changeable. In psychological terms, they take on an identity. Stewart Brand, in the *Whole Earth Software Catalog,* expressed it as follows:

> There are some 40,000 commercial programs for personal computers on the market, and they all work. Why not just grab the handiest and proceed? Because software, when it is used at all intensely, comes to feel like an extension of your nervous system. Its habits become your habits. The reason the term 'personal' got stuck to these machines is, they become part of your person.[8]

In other words, some software is better than others. Why? Because it becomes part of your person. The computer is not the same thing to all people; it has the ability to become an extension of one's personality. It also has the ability to change one's personality.

In Sherry Turkle's six year study of how children relate to computers she found that "each child developed a distinctive style of mastery," which she put into categories of hard and soft mastery. "The hard masters tend to see the world as something to be brought under control," whereas "the soft masters are more likely to see the world as something they need to accommodate to, something beyond their direct control."[9] Turkle described one child, Deborah's reaction to computers:

> Many people are lonely and isolated, but when they have a computer around it can feel like somebody is always there, always ready, always responsive, but without the responsibility of having to deal with another person. The computer offers a unique mixture of being alone and yet not feeling alone.[10]

She quotes another child named Bruce:

> I think of the computer as being perfect. People are imperfect, and that's the difference. As of now, when you put things into a computer you pretty much know what it is going to do. With people you never know. That's the point. . .[11]

There is another very important element. The information of the computer is of only one type, and that can have an impact on relationships. Jerry Mander wrote about this in terms of the computer being "opaque" to certain types of information:

> . . . computers, like television, are opaque to many kinds of information—sensory information, moods, feelings, meaning, context, among many others—is given little note or importance. And yet there are important consequences. Subtracting sensory information makes it difficult to communicate the nuances of nature and nature-based culture or to communicate human essence. Subtracting feeling leaves information, understanding and decision-making in the dry realm of the objective.[12]

Mander offers an illustration: the Canadian government's attempt to help the Inuit people of Northern Canada resist oil company incursion by giving them computers to keep track of wildlife. By using an information system similar to that of the oil companies, it was reasoned that the Inuit could better hold off development. The computer, however, viewed nature's patterns on an objective plane, calculating numbers and directions in terms of "cost benefit" or "animal units." The Native peoples were thus being asked to discard many other dimensions of information that were useful to them. As Mander concluded:

> The more powerful mythical, sensory, historic and spiritual relationships with creatures and the land, the dimensions which sustained the Inuit for thousands of years and make them different from you and me, will be amputated. In the end, I believe, the Inuit will begin to conceptualize the animals in the same way as the corporations, and Canada will have achieved something more than it originally suggested.[13]

To illustrate from another realm, consider the military, where computers are used, as Mander describes it, much like a "giant video game," with generals and technicians sitting in underground caverns looking at the various positions of weapons and targets, "following electronic blips on a massive screen—abstract, cerebral, removed from direct involvement at least until the things finally start exploding."[14] The human being's relationship to war changes from a personal encounter with a bayonet, rifle, or tank to impersonal blips on a screen. A crucial factor in this new computerized relationship is that the time available to make decisions has been shortened to minutes. The United States and the Soviet Union stand six minutes apart from the possibility of massive attack and retaliation. Multiple ways to accomplish each possibility are already programmed, and though it takes human involvement to start either event, once started, we have only a handful of minutes either to divert the plan or wait for impact. Worse, it is technically possible that humans could be dropped out of the decision loop altogether if programs were used that responded "automatically" to a certain set of prearranged happenings, such as the launch of missiles by one side or the other.

Many agree that it is not the computer that is the problem, it is the people. Yet as Mander argued:

> it is a simple fact that if there were no computers, the process of engaging in war would be a much more drawn-out proposition, with a lot more time for human beings to change their minds or seek alternatives. In fact, it is only because of computers that this virtually instant war—especially at the worldwide level, producing total annihilation—even enters the realm of possibility.[15]

So much for the argument that technology is neutral. When evaluating a technology we must consider the way it changes the circumstances of existence. That is, we must consider the "worst possible use of that technology." And if we find that it is holocaust, then that technology should, to use my terms, be labeled immoral, not neutral.

Power

With regard to power, the question is not that of speed or capacity, but the classic "who controls what?" In the case of the Inuit, traditional power was being taken away from them. Not only were the oil companies interested in their land (to satisfy the desires of people thousands of miles away) but computers were changing the ways they thought about the meaning of the animals on their land.

It is often touted that computers will change the officeplace as well as the voting booth. The office worker will be able to do everything and anything from a seated interaction with a keyboard and a screen. The citizen will be able to receive personalized information through interactive news systems and will be able to register choices in elections without leaving the home computer console. What is not often touted is the shift in power behind these scenarios. The question is not just who will benefit, but who will benefit most.

David Burnham, writing in *The Computer State*, had this to say:

> Power is the ability to persuade others by overt or covert means to do one's will. There are many different ways that the computer enhances the power of organizations. With the computer, organizations can collect large amounts of information about the current and past activities of individuals and groups . . . With the computer, organizations can analyze information about the activities, opinions and social characteristics of individuals in ways that allow them to anticipate the future actions, desires and fears of the groups of people with whom these individuals associate.[16]

So while on the one hand computer bureaucrats are talking about "improving communications" with their customers or constituents, Burnham is asking us to think about how the same communication methodology is "used to allow the people in control to say only what they already have determined their listeners want to hear." The relevant issue of power (control) is that such computer applications are "available only to the richest and most powerful institutions of our society."[17] The isolated citizen with a computer may be able to raise some hell through unauthorized entry into the sophisticated computer system of a powerful institution, but the citizen is no match for the nature and extent of equipment available to the centralized computer powers. Langdon Winner expressed it by an illustration: "Using a personal computer makes one no more powerful vis-a-vis, say, the U.S. National Security Agency than flying a hang glider establishes a person as a match for the U.S. Air Force."[18]

In classic economic fashion, larger businesses can afford larger computers than smaller businesses. And although small businesses are at a tremendous advantage when they use computers in their inventory, billing, payroll, taxes, etc., larger businesses can be involved with computers in a much wider range of activities: buying and selling, shipping, inventory control and market analysis. The end result is that larger businesses gain an edge and not only survive better, but often swallow up smaller, less efficient businesses. Thus the computerization of business is a technological change that supports giantism. Jerry Mander sees it as an unequal situation:

> . . . the computer is not in equal service to all parties. While you and your colleagues are networking about corporate behavior in a forest near you, that same corporation is moving information among thousands of its disparate pieces all over the world. The machine helps them more than it helps you. It's not neutral. And when a new, better computer is built, they will have it first.[19]

Alan F. Westin has written about the imbalance of power inherent in the fact that developing computer technology is very expensive. Of course there are cheap individual home computers available, but the catch, according to Westin, is that

> as long as the only people to build computerized record systems are those who use them to increase their own effectiveness, power, and influence, then we have increasingly a consolidation of power in society.[20]

Others, however, do hold out for the potential of individualizing the ability to use computers, considering especially ways they might be linked together into special networks. In writing about computers, Stewart Brand believes that "the human frame of reference is ashift." Whereas computers were tools first developed by large institutions, especially the military, the fact that every few years they become smaller and faster eventually led to developments by individuals. Brand feels that personal computers have shifted the power balance, and "it may be that more significant invention is coming from the hands of individuals."[21]

Sherry Turkle uses the following illustration in her book to support the notion that computers are of value because "the actual experience of using the machine offered a way to think about who one is and who one would like to be."[22]

> For some people the railroad signifies progress: for others it signifies the rape of nature. But either way, if you want to use the railroad, you have only one choice. You buy a ticket, get on the train, and let it take you to your destination.[23]

Her conclusion strikes me as somewhat romantic in the face of the massive institutional use of computers. She seems rather to suggest that unless "mindsets" change, we do not have a choice. In other words, through the power of massive information control those in power let you think it is your choice while they, in fact, determine the destination.

The way we think about ourselves

Overarching all the ins and outs of this kind of argument and feelings about what is good and bad is the issue of metaphor. And that is how I shall end this essay — with a thought from Dr. Joseph Weizenbaum, author of the superbly thought-provoking book, *Computer Power and Human Reason: From Judgment to Calculation.*

> One of the great dangers of the computer is its impact on the metaphoric way we think about ourselves. Just a few minutes ago in this room I heard someone talk about people being programmed. This shows the pervasiveness and perversity of the computer as a metaphor. It suggests that society is beginning to think of human beings as merely another species of the genus information processing system.[21]

Our language gives us away.

ENGINEERING THE ENGINEER: TECHNOLOGY TURNED INWARD

We went to the moon not
because of our technology but
because of our imagination.

Norman Cousins

Imagine: A mouse with six parents; patented life forms; the synthesis of a living cell; the synthesis of a gene; introducing a gene from a bacterium into a human cell and making it work.

Imagine these and you know only the past—what has already been done.

Imagine: two women plus no male producing one embryo, or two males plus no female producing one embryo, i.e, homosexual biological parenthood.

Imagine: watching the birth of a mammoth after taking the nucleus from a cell of a forty thousand year old frozen mammoth and implanting it into an elephant egg and then using an elephant mother for its development. Or imagine a newspaper headline, "Mummy Comes Back To Life" (genes from an Egyptian mummy cloned into life).

Imagine: taking present day genetic materials, unlocking the ancestral information in them and running evolution backwards to see where we came from.

Imagine these and you know the future—but only the future as it is being talked about now. Who knows what will be tried the day after tomorrow?

Correcting deficiencies, defects and diseases

Until now, we have applied our scientific knowledge and abilities to correct human deficiencies, defects and diseases. But the very success of that knowledge and research has raised a new question: should we attempt to improve the individual and the species by changing our physical and mental capabilities? That is, should we turn our technology inward? Should we experiment with ourselves for the purpose of achieving a significant upward change in the normal range of human capabilities and expectations?

When I was a boy I could have imagined something like a kidney transplant but I surely would not have been able to get one or make any kind of decision about one. Transplants just were not possible. But now they are. And people are making decisions that may appear to be routine, but by historical standards are surely miraculous. In 1972, when the United States Congress authorized Medicare to cover patients needing kidney dialysis and transplants, the expectation was about five thousand patients and a cost of 135 million dollars per year. By 1984, the number of patients was seventy thousand per year and the cost two billion and growing.

Biotechnological change was slow until the 1900's, when chemicals and machines mushroomed into an incredible array of techniques, tests and treatments. We have plunged at a dizzying pace into the production of heart pacemakers, heart-lung machines, artificial hips which can outlast us, penile implants, whole body scanners, EEG's, EKG's, you-name-it, there it is. We have whipped smallpox and have polio cornered. We have more drugs than a drugstore can stock or a doctor can remember. We transplant organs from the newly-dead to the dying. We even take all the blood out for some operations and put it back when surgery is over.

Bioengineering is a reality. In addition to new lifesaving machines, powerful and sophisticated methods are available to recombine genetic material from any living species, whether human, carrot or dolphin. Put simply, laboratory techniques can snip genetic material into small pieces and glue them back together into unique combinations never before seen in evolutionary history. Without mentioning specifics, the following general areas of bioengineering are being pursued:

— **pharmaceuticals:** shifting from the industrial synthesis of drugs, antibiotics, vaccines, hormones or enzymes to growing them by engineering new organisms;
— **mining:** creating microorganisms that produce enzymes that eat the metal salts in an ore to leave behind a pure metal;
— **energy:** creating new plants that are well-adapted to being used directly as a fuel or are easily converted into fuel;

— **agriculture:** increasing the photosynthetic efficiency of food plants; transferring nitrogen-fixing genes into food plants so that nitrogen fertilizers based on oil would no longer be needed; transferring into food plants genes that ward off viruses or pests;
— **animals:** bypassing slow natural breeding by programming new genetic traits directly into a fetus; crossing species boundaries to create new animals for specific economic demands; changing the genetics of grazing animals so they could get nourishment through carbohydrates in wood, or from a direct use of photosynthesis, feed themselves from the sun;
— **humans:** eliminating harmful genetic traits from a fetus; introducing genes that either alleviate a defect or that enhance physical or mental characteristics.

What life "knows" genetically can potentially be shared with all living species. Today the experiments are on cells. Tomorrow, organisms: human-made hybrids that cross what we used to think were inviolate genetic boundaries. Talk about going to school! Through genetic hybridization we can, in principle, learn everything "evolution" is now capable of doing. Maybe we can even devise a few new tricks and penetrate the biological and emotional roots of what it is to be a man or woman. But if we set out to cure ourselves of our limitations, should we not also wonder what genetic pollution would be like? How would genetic potential be balanced with genetic pollution?

Jeremy Rifkin, in his author's note to *Algeny*, captured the issue very well:

> While the nation has begun to turn its attention to the dangers of nuclear war, little or no debate has taken place over the emergence of an entirely new technology that in time could very well pose as serious a threat at the existence of life on this planet as the bomb itself. With the arrival of bioengineering, humanity approaches a crossroads in its own technological history. It will soon be possible to engineer and produce living systems by the same technological principles we now employ in our industrial processes. The wholesale engineering of life, in accordance with technological prerequisites, design specifications, and quality controls, raises fundamental questions.[1]

The importance of the discovery of fire is being matched in our time by the discovery of DNA. Whereas we used fire to create new materials, we will use DNA to create new beings. The engineer is about to engineer the engineer.

Novelist David Baltimore summed it up:

> We're close to being able to learn just about anything we want to know about molecular genetics. I know that's an audacious statement. But we're at the point now that if we know how to ask the question, the methods are there to answer it—although it may take years or decades . . . Thus in the foreseeable future, we will understand cancer, genetic disease . . . and the development and function of the nervous system.[2]

Experimental contact with ourselves

"Technology turned inward" is experimental contact with ourselves—a kind of merging of two imperatives: the imperative of technology that says if you can do it, do it, and the imperative of medicine that if you can relieve suffering, do it. Such a merging brings forth today the historically unique question of species identity. Ever since Rachel Carson's 1962 book *Silent Spring,* we have become more and more aware of species survival. Ecology, environment, and pollution are familiar terms. Will we foul our own nest so much that we, too, as a species, go the way of extinction? The issue of the survival of species demands our best attention. But what about the question of species identity? Should we experiment with ourselves so we will change into a new and different species?

We have two links with our past: our culture and our genes. History provides the record of how cultures have waxed and waned, how they have gotten out of order. No culture has sustained itself through history without significant change. Indeed, most distinct historical cultures have disappeared! Biology, on the other hand, is becoming a record of our battles over our genetic heritage—and its future. One hopes that we are gaining the knowledge to survive our environmental disasters, but we are also gaining the knowledge that will give us the power to decide what to do about our genes—in terms of which ones we like and which ones we do not. Perhaps we will be able to generate genes never before known in evolutionary history! In short, we face the power to decide what kind of genetic future we want.

Some people hesitate: after all, they say, we really have a long way to go, things are quite complicated and it may be hundreds of years until we are able to make a big impact on our genetics. I suggest that people who believe this read up on genetics in general science magazines—*Science News, Science, Scientific American,* etc.

They will soon realize that the speed of genetic advances is mind-boggling even to those involved.

I also suggest that they ponder an imaginary analogy concerning the nature of change in a technologically-dominated world. The analogy is between flying and genetics. Sixty-six years elapsed between Kitty Hawk, North Carolina and Tranquility Base, Moon—1903 to 1969. Now imagine standing on the sand dunes of Kitty Hawk in 1903 telling the Wright brothers that even though humans had dreamed of flying from time immemorial, now that they had done it, we would be flying to the moon in sixty-six years. Nuts, you would have been. In 1953 the genetic code was "cracked" when James Watson and Francis Crick published a paper on the helical structure of the DNA molecule. If we add sixty-six years to that, we get to the year 2019. Imagine going up to Watson and Crick in their lab in 1953 and telling them that by 2019 there would be a new species of humans designed by humans! If genetic technology can make the kind of progress that aeronautical engineering made in one lifetime, then within the lifetime of many reading this essay, the human species will produce its successor.

Impossible? So was flying to the moon. You see, science and technology regard questions of genetic change as practical, not philosophical questions. Is there not abundant proof in this past century that once a scientific question is asked, the answer is soon forthcoming? José Delgado, the eminent brain researcher, has seriously suggested that the time has come in human history to accept a major new universal goal: the development of ourselves, not our machines.

Doing something good

With respect to genetic technology there are two major issues that will not be discussed here. The first is safety: what would happen if recombinant DNA techniques produced a new organism that created a new epidemic when let loose in the environment? The second is commercialism: the economic exploitation of patented organisms—a variation of the slavery issue. For example, it is now possible to exclusively own organisms that consume oil, as well as vegetables like okra, celery or cucumbers grown from genetically-tailored seeds.

The issue that will be discussed is that of direction—the direction of the good. We now know how to transplant a functioning gene from one species of mammal to another. The immediate goal is to alleviate the tragic effects of genetic diseases such as Tay-Sachs or diabetes. But what about dreaming of "gene therapy," or a transfer of gene complexes relating to emotional, mental or physical abilities? Should we cross the therapeutic line to work on the side of attempted improvements?

In gene transplant experiments there is no intention other than that of doing something good, relieving suffering. But we are, after all human. And that should give us some pause to wonder. To borrow an image from Archie and Edith Bunker:

Archie: That's you, all right. "Edith the Good!" You'll stoop to anything to be good. You never yell, you never swear. You never make nobody mad. You think it's easy livin' with a saint? Even when you cheat, you don't cheat to win. You cheat to lose! You ain't human!
Edith: That's a terrible thing to say, Archie Bunker. I'm just as human as you are.
Archie: Oh, yeah . . . then prove you're just as human as me. Do somethin' rotten.[3]

"Do somethin' rotten." As we develop genetic technology, we must keep in mind the human propensity for evil. Or the way we inadvertently do "wrong"—even with the best of intentions. A friend told me once that perhaps we will have to develop "whoops ethics" to take care of any problems.

Biologists, for example, have transplanted a human gene into the pink petunia. As the petunias grow, the transplanted gene secretes minute quantities of a female reproductive hormone, thus offering the commercial hope of huge flower beds producing a cash crop of valuable chemicals as well as aesthetic beauty. All of which seems fine, given our industrialized mindset toward production. But what if the mindset changes from petunias as mini-factories to the production of genes or gene combinations that affect human emotions or intelligence? The troublesome part is that biology has entered the economic marketplace where the emphasis is on making as much money as possible in the shortest time. Hardly a value to wish for in relation to changes in our genetic make-up! In the 1980's, small genetic engineering companies began to appear on the scene, gambling that new profits would come from rearranging genes. They now number over three hundred, with new ones starting and old ones failing monthly. With the investment level reaching into the billions, the business competition drive is on. But the subject is nothing less than life! The U.S. Food and Drug Administration has already approved over forty applications of genetic engineering for disease diagnosis. The U.S. Patent Office has received over one thousand applications for biotechnology. The race is on.

I do not intend to make a straight line correlation, but it would be well to remember the impact of the transfer of complete biological entities into new environments. To cite just one example, the Asian fungus which wiped out the American chestnut was imported on nursery plants. The principle is that introduction of radical newness into biological sytems can cause radical change. Even though we cannot predict the changes, changes there will surely be as we introduce new genes into new organisms. If a major motivation is to make money, the odds for drastic mistakes certainly increase.

Not to mention the matter of "new life for new weapons." In other words, where is the military in all this? Already the United States and the Soviet Union have been posturing in the newspapers, accusing each other of engaging in genetic engineering for biological warfare. The inevitable phrase "gene gap" has been touted as the reason for "defensive" research. The stage is set for a repeat in the biological arena of the succession of military "gaps" that has propelled the world into a massive arms race. The stage is set for the creation of a contagious flu virus that creates cobra venom in the human system. You see, there are more military weapons than missiles and tanks. The same biological technology that has the potential for producing an end to genetic disease also has the potential for introducing new ways to die.

The poor have genes too

In the light of current technological problems in the areas of energy, consumer-based production, agriculture and the military, we have an ethical responsibility to ask what impact genetic technology will have on the peoples of less-developed countries. Will this kind of technology lift their burdens or add to them? Let us remember that the clarion call for technology that we have heard since World War II has almost singlemindedly promoted technologies that will lift burdens. Only recently have we been willing to consider the ways in which the use of technology has burdened the poor.

Daniel Callahan of the Hastings Institute has outlined three ethical justifications for proceeding with the acquisition of new knowledge. The first is *individual liberty*—the right to seek that which one desires if there is no demonstrable harm to others. The second is *risk-benefit*—comparing the risks taken and the benefits expected, with the moral action determined by how one outweighs the other. The third is *doing good*—the idea that it is better to try to do good than to try to avoid harm. These justifications are amply supported by the writings of many profound thinkers in human history, as well as by practical examples of human action. But what I think is most significant about Callahan's attempt to organize justification is what he says after this.

> The problem is that, taken together, they seem to lead to predictable, almost preordained outcomes. They do not allow us in any fashion to pose larger questions about the nature of human happiness, the most appropriate and valuable direction which science as a whole should take, or to inquire about the best ends to which human freedom should be directed.[4]

In other words, these justifications are utilitarian in the sense that they deal only with action and not direction. Thus Callahan goes on:

> . . . their only effect on genetic engineering has been to bring about a short-term moratorium in one case, that of recombinant DNA research. Otherwise, the research has gone on . . . But doesn't this beg the question? . . . It is precisely the sameness of the outcome of the application of the three principles noted above which renders them suspect.[5]

The punch line is the next sentence: "They simply cannot be the right principles if they lead only to decisions to carry on the research."[6]

In other words, the question, "Are there some things we can do that we should not?" has not been asked by those involved in the technology or the ethics. Asking the question has not led anyone to ask, in turn, why? Why is our society interested in genetic change? But we find ourselves full-blown into the development of new technologies. Yet shouldn't we first discuss social goals and then consider what techniques and technologies we need? Especially in the case of genetic technology, with its potential for basic structural changes in our very species?

As Robert Sinsheimer has posed the question:

> Do we want to assume the basic responsibility for life on this planet—to develop new living forms for our own purpose? Shall we take into our hands our own future evolution?[7]

And what will the poor have to say about it? Shall they be asked to eat their genetic cake too?

Can science recognize love?

Historian Theodore Roszak has approached this matter from the perspective of Mary Shelley's *Frankenstein,* calling science to recognize something that it does not at present: love. Referring to Dr. Frankenstein's project, Roszak observed:

> Where did the doctor's great project go wrong? Not in his intentions, which were beneficient, but in the dangerous haste and egotistic myopia with which he pursued his goal. It is both a beautiful and a terrible aspect of our humanity, this capacity to be carried away by an idea. For all the best reasons, Victor Frankenstein wished to create a new and improved human type. What he knew was the secret of his creature's physical assemblage; he knew how to manipulate the material parts of nature to achieve an astonishing result. What he did not know was the secret of personality in nature. Yet he raced ahead, eager to play God, without knowing God's most divine mystery. So he created something that was soulless. And when that monstrous thing appealed to him for the one gift that might redeem it from monstrosity, [making him a mate], Frankenstein discovered to his horror that, for all his genius, it was not within him to provide that gift. Nothing in his science comprehended it. The gift was love. The doctor knew everything there was to know about his creature—except how to love it as a person.[8]

Given the history of science it seems ludicrous to ask scientists to consider the gift of love as they explore the universe. But when the exploration turns to genetic manipulation and the stakes are human existence itself, how can we leave out such human qualities as love? To proceed in the direction of changing the person, what of the person must we take into account? Roszak goes on to comment on what scientists fail to understand:

The reason one despairs of discussing "alternative cognitive systems" with scientists is that scientists inevitably want an alternative system to do exactly what science already does—to produce predictive, manipulative information about the structure and function of nature—only perhaps to do so more prolifically and more rapidly. What they fail to understand is that no amount of information on earth would have taught Victor Frankenstein how to redeem his flawed creation from monstrosity.[9]

Should scientists be the only ones allowed to control genetic engineering? How does the rest of the human community feel about where we ought to go, what we ought to do to ourselves, by whom we should be replaced? In what way should we take into account the reality of love as expressed by Paul in I Corinthians 13: "I may have all knowledge and understand all secrets; I may have all the faith needed to move mountains—but if I have no love I am nothing." If love is something to strive for, how can we act out its attributes: be patient and kind, not jealous or selfish, not happy with evil, but happy with the truth? In short, how, through our technology, can we act out love as servants?

Jeremy Rifkin puts the issue in terms of the blend of science and religious consciousness, of the tension between the created and the creator. He writes: "Our children will be convinced that their creations are of a far superior nature to those from which they were copied . . . Our children will view their imitation of nature as nature."[10] And further:

Nature is being made anew, this time by human beings. We no longer feel ourselves to be guests in someone else's home and therefore obliged to make our behavior conform with a set of preexisting cosmic rules. It is our creation now. We make the rules. We establish the parameters of reality. We create the world, and because we do, we no longer feel beholden to outside forces. We no longer have to justify our behavior, for we are now the architects of the universe. We are responsible to nothing outside ourselves, for we are the kingdom, the power, and the glory for ever and ever.[11]

Shall we say, Amen? Or begin to talk about science and love?

SIX

BEFRIENDING MOUNT EVEREST:
THE NUCLEAR GENIE

The Easterner talks about conquering Mount Everest. The Taoist talks about befriending Mount Everest. There is a difference, and our language gives us away.

Rain dances and seeding clouds

Yes, and there is a difference between a rain dance and seeding clouds. Morris Berman, in *The Reenchantment of the World*, compares the two:

> When the Indian does a rain dance, for example, he is not assuming an automatic response. There is no failed technology here, rather, he is inviting the clouds to join him, to respond to the invocation. He is, in effect, asking to make love to them, and like any normal lover they may or may not be in the mood. *This is the way nature works.* By means of this approach, the native learns about the reality of the situation, the moods of the earth and the skies. He surrenders. . . . Western technology, on the other hand, seeds the clouds by airplanes. It takes nature by force, 'masters' it, has no time for mood or subtlety, and thus, along with the rain, we get noise, pollution, and the potential disruption of the ozone layer. Rather than put ourselves in harmony with nature, we seek to conquer it, and the result is ecological destruction.[1]

To conquer a mountain is to see relationships as competitive and exploitative, whereas to befriend a mountain sees them as collaborative and convivial. "The working assumption," writes Wendell Berry,

> has been that nature and society, like laboratory experiments, can be manipulated by processes that are for the most part comprehensible toward ends that are for the most part foreseeable. But the analogy, as any farmer would know instantly, is too simple, for both nature and humanity are vast in possibility, unpredictable and ultimately mysterious.[2]

And thus it is, Berry says in another essay, that "the energy crisis is not a crisis of technology but of morality."[3] The Western relationship with nature has been to see it only as a source for fuel, as "extractable energy." The issue, then, is not one of fuels but one of restraint, and the energy crisis is reduced to a single question: Can we hold back from doing everything we are able to do?

Improving nature: equilibrium and wizardry

The topics of energy and agriculture need considerable rethinking in the light of technology and values. As long as we continue to operate out of the framework that nature is ours to use, not share, and that the way out of technological problems is more of the same kind of technology, we are doomed to make the situation worse. Embedded in our technologies of energy and agriculture is the notion of our improving nature. What we can control, we can change and improve. As naturalist and poet Loren Eiseley once put it with tongue-in-cheek eloquence:

> This is the great age, make no mistake about it; the robot has been born somewhat appropriately along with the atom bomb, and the brain they say now is just another type of more complicated feedback system. The engineers have its basic principles worked out; it's mechanical, you know, nothing to get superstitious about; and man can always improve on nature once he gets the idea.[4]

In our rush toward control and change we have lost contact with the notion of equilibrium. We have in many ways turned into machines, yet we have forgotten that all machines need adjustment and can break down when run too hard or long. In a novel about wizardry and the "crafts of finding, binding, mending, unsealing and revealing," Ursula K. LeGuin points to the issue of balance in an exchange between Ged, the apprentice, and the Master Hand, the master wizard of illusion. Ged wants to know how to make changes permanent. And the Master Hand answers:

> This is a rock . . . a little bit of the dry land on which men live. It is itself. It is part of the world. By the Illusion-Change you can make it look like a diamond—or a flower or a fly or an eye or a flame—' The rock flickered from shape to shape as he named them, and returned to rock. 'But that is mere seeming . . . it does not change the thing. To change this rock into a jewel . . . is to change the world. It can be done. Indeed it can be done. It is the art of the Master Changer, and you will learn it, when you are ready to learn it.[5]

Then the Master Hand gets to the point:

> But you must not change one thing, one pebble, one grain of sand, until you know what good and evil will follow on the act. The world is in balance, in Equilibrium. A wizard's power of Changing and Summoning can shake the balance of the world. It is dangerous, that power. It is most perilous. It must follow knowledge, and serve need. To light a candle is to cast a shadow . . .[6]

The allegorical image of technology as wizardry is clear: to light a candle is to cast a shadow. To change something is to create consequences. The wisdom of the Master Hand is that learning to listen for the future echo of the consequences is a responsibility we must learn if we are to serve need.

Nuclear weapons and repentance

Actually all this is a somewhat lengthy, but necessary introduction to the matter of nuclear technology, whether for energy or for weapons. And to tell the end of the story right off: we can do without both. Indeed if we do not, we forfeit our future.

The first controlled chain reaction of nuclear fission in 1942 not only verified the reality of a radically new physical phenomenon, it also set in motion the need for a chain reaction, if you will, in the human arena of social and political affairs. With the explosion of the atom bomb over Hiroshima just three years later, the age-old concept of war died. As Pope John Paul II said in a February, 1981 speech in Hiroshima:

> In the past, it was possible to destroy a village, a town, a region, even a country. Now it is the whole planet that has come under threat. This fact should fully compel everyone to face a basic moral consideration: from now on, it is only through a conscious choice and then deliberate policy that humanity can survive.[7]

Such words are not rhetoric or the result of an over-zealous imagination. The fact is simply that the planet is now computer-missile wired with some fifty thousand nuclear weapons capable of killing all humans some twenty times over if all were detonated in one gory finale to a human dispute or accident. Jonathan Schell has commented that the Pope's words distinguished "between 'a conscious choice' and 'deliberate policy.'"[8] In other words, there are two stages to pass through with regard to the nuclear predicament. One is individual and spiritual and the other is public and political. What may well be unprecedented is that we must deal with both at the same time. It is like two plays on one stage at the same time. We are called to make sense of the spiritual *and* the political as one.

When we consider the effects of nuclear explosions of the magnitude now available, it literally defies the imagination because it is so far removed from any human experience. In *The Fate of the Earth,* Schell outlined five destructive effects:[9]

1) initial nuclear radiation: one medium-size weapon would kill all unprotected humans within an area of six square miles;

2) electromagnetic pulse: intense gamma radiation would knock out all electrical equipment over a wide area; one Defense Department estimate is that one multi-kiloton nuclear weapon detonated 125 miles above a midwestern city would damage solid-state electrical circuits throughout the continental United States and parts of Mexico and Canada;

3) thermal pulse: the ten-second wave of blinding light and intense heat from a one-megaton bomb would cause second-degree burns in exposed humans at a distance of nine and a half miles;

4) blast wave: a one-megaton bomb would flatten or seriously damage buildings up to a radius of four and a half miles;

5) radioactive fallout: varying according to whether the bomb ex-

plodes in the air or on the ground, the average estimate is that a one-megaton bomb would contaminate over a thousand square miles with a lethal dose for half the able-bodied young adult population.

Keep in mind that the estimate for the total global megatonnage of nuclear weapons is in excess of ten thousand, not one . . . and rising as new weapons are made. It borders on the absurd. And if the list above is not enough, consider that in 1982, top-quality scientists in the United States and the Soviet Union made known their calculations on the prospects of a "nuclear winter." As Schell summarized it:

> The earth—its cities and its forests in particular—is like a well-laid fire. If you light it with enough nuclear matches, it will burn, and as it burns it will fill the atmosphere with smoke and plunge much of the world into a frigid darkness for several months.[10]

In a worst-case scenario of ten thousand megatons of nuclear "matches" being struck in one exchange, the temperatures in the Northern Hemisphere could sink to twenty-three degrees below zero, Fahrenheit. The biological consequences are enormous, ranging from inhibition of photosynthesis in ocean algae and tropical forests to the total disruption of the biological base for human survival.

Schell spelled out in *The Fate of the Earth* the quandary of our desire for all this to go away, knowing it will not. Yet if it does not, we will not be around because it has happened.

> When one tries to face the nuclear predicament, one feels sick, whereas when one pushes it out of mind, as apparently one must do most of the time in order to carry on with life, one feels well again. But this feeling of well-being is based on a denial of the most important reality of our time, and therefore is itself a kind of sickness.[11]

He went on next to point to society:

> A society that systematically shuts its eyes to an urgent peril to its physical survival and fails to take any steps to save itself cannot be called psychologically well. In effect, whether we think about nuclear weapons or avoid thinking about them, their presence among us makes us sick, and there seems to be little of a purely mental or emotional nature that we can do about it.[12]

I do not intend to persuade you to accept a specific solution because the direction is inward first . . . what your own experience of love, reconciliation and, finally, repentance is. And I certainly understand that in nuclear matters, the solution is not unilateral. The reality is that two superpowers are locked in a nuclear arm-wrestling match and neither shows any sign of backing down. They never will until enough individuals look inward and then help our societies to do that also. I will say only one thing about the Soviet Union. One thing because it is the most important thing to begin to ponder inwardly. George Kennen, former United States Ambassador to the Soviet Union, wrote in 1982 about learning to see the behavior of the Soviet leaders partly as a reflection of our own behavior:

> If we insist on demonizing these Soviet leaders   on viewing them as total and incorrigible enemies, consumed only with their fear or hatred of us and dedicated to nothing other than our destruc-tion — then, in the end, that is the way we shall assuredly have them — if for no other reason than that our view of them allows for nothing else — either for them or for us [13]

To pray seriously and deeply over Kennen's words is a must if we are to engender any hope, any movement away from the nu-clear brink.

In a peculiar combination of words, "preemptive repentance," Schell has suggested an interesting combination for Christian con-cern and technology.

> To combine strategic with Christian terminology, we must adopt a policy of preemptive repentance. We must repent the crime before we commit it, and in that repentance find the will not to commit it. This displacement of repentance from the aftermath of the crime to the time preceeding it would be, to paraphrase William James, the moral equivalent of deterrence. The only dif-ference between it and the strategic sort is that whereas *in strategic deterrence we are deterred by what the enemy may do to us, in moral deterrence we are deterred by what we may do to him* — and to countless innocents, including all potential future generations of human beings.[14]

In the time of the generations of Noah the Lord saw that the wickedness of humankind was great on the earth and that the imagination of human hearts was continually evil. Although I would not overlook the good and love that often prevail, there is much today to suggest that through a combination of technological prowess and economic greed we have sorely damaged the planet on which we live. We are tottering on the brink of brutal destruction—all because the imaginations of our hearts are imaginations of fear and not of sharing.

As is so well known to us from the Noah story, the corruption of the earth and of human beings was so great that God determined to make an end to all flesh. And so God caused the flood to come. The waters covered even the highest mountain and every living thing on the face of the earth was blotted out—except for Noah and the ark housing his family and the two-by-two remnants of every beast and bird according to its kind.

After the terrible destruction of life by the flood, God made a covenant with Noah and his descendants "that never again shall all flesh be cut off by the waters of a flood, and never again shall there be a flood to destroy the earth." (Genesis 9:11, Revised Standard Version). Our problem today, however, is not that God has turned away from that promise. Our problem is that humans in their age-old quest to play God have now achieved the God-power to destroy life. Nuclear war is not another kind of war. Nuclear weapons are not sticks grown up into stones, or stones grown up into swords, or swords grown up into rifles, or rifles grown up into cannons, or cannons grown up into bombers, or bombers grown up into missiles. Nuclear weapons carry with them the power of flood that made an end to all the flesh of the earth.

God will not do us in. It is *we* who might!

Nuclear energy is for history, not the future

Look at the problems with regard to nuclear energy:

(1) What about a nuclear plant accident similar to or worse than Three Mile Island? One can find all kinds of estimates, but the incredible part is people are trying to guess "when" and ignore the fact that the "when" they are talking about is a horrendous event.

(2) What about the costs? Is nuclear-generated electricity really cheap? Again, one can find all kinds of estimates, but where do we take into account the fact that whereas it was once touted that a generating plant would cost a few tens of millions of dollars, their

price tags continue to escalate and are now multi-billions of dollars each? Never mind that these billions need to be paid largely on the front end before any energy is produced. Never mind that the multi-billion dollar price tags do not include the cost of dismantling a plant when it has worn out in ten to twenty years. Estimates of plants being decommissioned today indicate that these cost will be equal to or more than the cost of building them in the first place.

(3) What about the radioactive wastes? If there had to be one sufficient reason to stop the development of more nuclear reactors it would be this one. The simple scientific fact is there is no way yet known to handle radioactive wastes other than storing them in containers that will have to be changed when they begin to leak. The storage time required ranges from a few days to a few hundred thousand years. All efforts to find ways to store radioactive wastes in the ocean or underground have been shown to be ineffective—a more honest word would be dangerous. Should we continue to pile up wastes, hoping that the race will be won by a solution instead of by an irreparable natural disaster? Which leads to the next question . . .

(4) How much radiation is dangerous? Here again, scientific estimates vary all over the ballpark. What is truly incredible is that the only way we can get the data is to expose people and see. There is no way to calculate the threshold dose of radiation below which there is no problem, above which there is a problem. We will get an answer, however, because people are being exposed more and more as more and more nuclear waste is produced. And where will we avert our eyes in shame if the "answer" turns out to be that we have passed the threshold of radiation exposure—if we realize there should be less radiation exposure but that we are already being exposed to that amount and more?

(5) Finally, what about the kind of society that would support wide-scale use of nuclear energy? The production of electricity by nuclear means requires sophisticated, complex facilities requiring highly-trained specialists to maintain and operate. In social terms, nuclear power plants are possible only in highly-centralized economic and political settings. There is no such thing as neighborhood control of, or even input to the management of a nuclear power plant. Nuclear development requires a "rigid" institutional, economic and social setting because the knowledge is so specialized and complex. A few people will be in control, either because they are the ones

who have the nuclear knowledge or because they are instrumental in the economic plan.

With problems like these our choice must be to let nuclear energy be a part of our history, but no more of our future.

Are there limits?

In a theological reflection on nuclear development, Jacques Ellul argues that whether we are talking about the production of energy or weapons, the theological questions raised are enough to make us stop.[15] The usual argument is that we should not stand in the way of scientific research, but Ellul turns the question around and asks: "Do we, before God, have the right to do absolutely nothing in protest of a type of research simply because it is scientific?" Or to put it a different way, "Are there limits? Is it good that science recognizes no limit?" In the area of atomic research, Ellul argues that "if it were simply a matter of knowing the constitution of matter, there would be no problem." As it turns out, what we end up with is not just knowledge but a kind of manipulation and transformation that has "no respect for either the Creator or the creation." "Yes, says Ellul, we do have to protest when we attempt to substitute ourselves for God. One example of this is the kind of spirit that motivates nuclear technology: we want "to pursue to the nth degree everything that can satisfy our spirit of power." Even in the face of monumental risks and unknowns we plunge ahead, confident that in the nick of time technology will solve its problems.

If one objects to nuclear energy, the historical shadows of the Luddites* and of Galileo get trotted out—and what can one say? What one can reply is that the questions are not *just* scientific. They are questions for the human spirit as well as for the human mind. They are questions of our images of the quality of life as well as questions of economic needs—whether making money or producing goods and services. They are questions of responsibility as well. As Ellul put it: "We are called to act as responsible beings, and the central question remains: 'What have you done to your sister and brother?'"

If we say we did not mean to have a nuclear plant break down and release significant radioactive pollution, that we did not mean

*Followers of Ned Ludd, who during England's Industrial Revolution attacked labor-saving machinery in factories.

to make energy so expensive, that we did not mean to let all those radioactive wastes leak out and cause irreparable damage and that we did not mean to increase the rate of cancer because radiation became a human-generated part of the environment, then we say we have not concerned ourselves with our sister and brother. Such an answer would be a denial of God's calling. The problem is, even though all this nuclear development is taking place in the arena of science, its impact is in the arena of people's lives. We seem paralyzed, unable to say no, or even to ask for a slowing down until more basic knowledge is available. Ellul says it bluntly: "If we do not know what we are doing, we must not do it." Just imagine saying that to scientists!

There are alternatives

What cannot be overlooked in the nuclear arena is that *there are options. There are alternatives.* There are different paths we can take, paths not back into the past or returning to the Stone Age. One is the path of nuclear disarmament—not all weapons, but the nuclear ones. This would involve coming to our senses that with nuclear weapons the chances of total global destruction are ever-present and sooner or later . . . Another option is the path of solar energy. This would mean coming to our senses that there already exists a source of energy that is free, does not pollute, is abundant beyond any conceived level of use and that, unbelievably, is renewable since it comes to the earth every single day. The technology of solar energy does not need further development in order to justify its use. What is needed is human economic willingness and interest to seek its growth through the retooling of the earth to solar energy instead of forcing more development for nuclear, coal, gas or oil. We already know how to use the sun for any energy need we have devised. We do not yet have the will to do it. I know, unfortunately, from many years' experience of teaching about solar energy, that most people will not believe me. But that is a problem of brainwashing, not of knowledge. All one has to do is look up the literature on solar energy and see what is there. All one has to do is be open to the fact that we are basically "sot in our ways" and tend to believe only what we have been brought up on: coal, gas, oil and, since World War II, the promise of nuclear energy.

Nuclear technology and sin

In a strange but important way it does not seem overzealous to me to ponder the possibility that using nuclear technology puts humans into the situation of sin. Since most of us relate sin to personal behavior, to think of sin in relation to technology may seem at first inappropriate, if not perverse.

My understanding of sin, however, comes from Romans 5 and 6. I see sin as anything that prevents us from realizing God's purpose for our lives. In New Testament terms, I understand God's purpose for us is to love the world as Christ did, a love stemming from servanthood, not control. In Old Testament terms, I understand God's purpose to be for us to obey God's commandments. God forbidding Adam and Eve to eat the fruit of the tree in the garden was not a warning to stay away from a poisonous fruit; it was not God exercising "parental control" by establishing yes'es and no's. It was a statement of relationship. It made clear that there is a difference between God and humans and that we need to take that seriously.

We often get mixed up by not distinguishing sin from guilt, which is our awareness of sin. As skilled as we are at submerging our guilt, what really matters is sin. Sin, not guilt, disrupts the relationship between God and ourselves as chosen people. Moreover we find it hard to accept our need for God's help in overcoming our sin. In Romans 7, Paul wrote that sin is a power operative in every human person. He claimed that only God's miraculous deliverance in Christ liberates us and thereby allows us to live a new kind of life. Or as phrased in Romans 6:13, sin means the human inability to put themselves at God's disposal, to respond to God's will.

If it all boils down to the will of God, then we must ask the question: what *is* that will? James 4:17 offers a practical view: if we know what is right and fail to do it, that is sin. The will of God for us is to know and do what is right as Jesus taught by his own example. We read it in Matthew 25, about feeding the hungry and clothing the naked; in Jesus telling Nicodemus that he must be born again; in Mary's song of praise (Luke 1)—especially about remembering the lowly; in the reference to the first being last and the last first; and all the way to the end of Revelations, with the profound call of grace: "Come, whoever is thirsty; accept the water of life as a gift, whoever wants it." To fail to do any of these things is to break our relationship with God.

I believe that whether they are used to produce bombs or electricity, nuclear technologies are not "right". They are not right because they place incredible, lasting burdens on all creation. On the one hand, they cause us to live under the threat of global destruction through explosions of little suns released on earth. On the other hand, they produce prodigious quantities of radioactive wastes that must be stored away for tens of thousands of years. And because we reject other viable options — like nuclear disarmament and solar energy — we fail to do the right. Sin, it's called.

The questions staring at us are not questions of economics or electricity or deterrence. The fundamental nuclear question is this: can we separate the use of nuclear technology from our covenant with God? Doing away with nuclear technologies — and using the alternatives already available — would be a reasonable choice in the same sense as our choosing not to put into food chemicals that cause cancer.

SEVEN

CAN THE POOR PEOPLE GET A ROBOT TOO?

At a Hawaii 2000 conference in Honolulu in 1970, science-fiction writer Arthur C. Clarke gave a talk on the technological future. One of the persons who heard him was Alfred Pasatiempo, Sr., formerly a laborer with the State Highway Department. Although Clarke disavowed any credentials as a predictor of the future, Pasatiempo's response made him sound as if he had heard the words of a prophet.

> It's amazing what I learned . . . I sure would like to get one robot in my house. You know, we poor people like to live it up, too. In the morning instead of going to work I just push a button, and there it is. Then I push a button and I see my friend on the Mainland. The guy said you can talk to him so close like in your living room.
> I'll say, "Hey, bruddah! How's Los Angeles?" But I was wondering, can we afford it? I mean, how much is the down payment going to be? Can the poor people get a robot, or just the rich people?[1]

Given the way things work today, why ask such an inane question? What Peruvian peasant has had a kidney transplant? How many credit card holders are there among the faithful that crowd the Ganges river every day?

Technology is not neutral

The major thesis of this essay is that in any technological change we make there must be a connection to the poor. It is not enough to recognize that our present technologies do not take into account the human scale, or that there is more emphasis on quantity than on quality. It is not enough to make a better effort to see that the poor benefit from technology. What is needed is a different technology — one that takes into account the existence of the poor.

The notion of "trickle down," which means that as the rich get richer the poor will also improve their lot, is a notion that will not solve the gap between the existence of the rich and the existence of the poor. As John V. Taylor sees it

> Growth economy is interested in profits, not products; it seeks to reduce labour costs, not to create jobs. . . There is something extraordinarily cynical in the argument that the best way to feed the poor is to pile even more upon the rich man's table in the hope that bigger and better crumbs will fall from it.[2]

As it turns out: "What falls from the rich man's table is not crumbs but poisons and plastics."[3] Technological development has not been neutral.

It is hard to understand and so easy to forget that I am part of a minority group in the world. There are vastly more unlike me than like me, for the majority of people on this planet live in poverty. The majority human culture is that of being poor. What would it do to my self-image, for example, if my job was to stand in a *sanitario masculino* in a Rio de Janeiro airport and pull paper towels for the men who came in to wash their hands? Every time I see the men with that job I see a powerful metaphor for the message of development. To the poor, the uneducated, and the rural development says: Come to the city. Join us where we are with the money. Come inside the gate. But Jesus, we recall, is the one who went outside the gate.

The power of technology is as much in its demand that things be done its way as in the actual impact of technology itself. Our attitude toward the non-industrialized is like that of Mulla Nasrudin in the following story:

> One day Mulla found a tortoise. He tied it to his belt and continued his work in the fields. The tortoise started to struggle. The Mulla held it up and asked: 'What's the matter, don't you want to learn how to plough?'[4]

Do it our way, we tell the poor. Do it our way, even though we will not let you do all the things we do. Let us take care of the knowledge; you can deal with the problems. What is hard to understand and easy to forget is the relentlessness of poverty and the awesome power that keeps the poor poor.

To illustrate this in another way, consider the opening sentence of an article that appeared on the front page of a newspaper in 1985: "A statewide intensive care system credited with saving the lives of more than 300 infants a year is in danger of coming apart because it costs too much."[5] The article goes on to detail that four medical centers in Georgia reported 10.7 million dollars in annual unpaid bills for their newborn intensive care units. As a result, city-based hospitals in Georgia were pulling out of the statewide system of intensive care nurseries for newborns. Worse, hospitals were beginning to turn away newborns if their families did not have insurance or the ability to pay bills averaging twelve thousand dollars per baby. On the other hand, it was reported that those who could pay bills or who had insurance were going more and more to private, for-profit hospitals with intensive care units.

The bottom line is that the poor get left out. Does it not seem bizarre to go to great lengths in research and education to develop medical technologies for saving lives and then to place the technologies in an economic setting that prices them out of the reach of all except a privileged few? Technology thus ends up improving or saving the lives of fewer and fewer people. Although it is utopian even to think it, would it not be a fascinating world indeed if the prevailing ethic and reality was that the best possible health care ought to be available at the least possible cost? What if a kidney dialysis machine were the cost of a portable tape recorder?

Have you ever wondered why medical technology costs so much? I certainly know all the arguments about the sophistication of the equipment, about the magnitude and complexity of medical education. Such traditional arguments, however, must be placed alongside the undeniable fact that the development and use of medical technology machines and the entire delivery system of health care is going in an economic direction that results in more and more being available to fewer and fewer people. Is there any hope that the ideas and skills needed to change our lifestyles might be expanded in order to improve our health? But how are the poor of the world even going to be able to do that, when they already have less food and live in environments filled with conditions that degrade health?

It seems perverse to argue against the development of technologies to help newborn babies, but there is another fundamental issue that cannot be avoided: simply, are we going to save every baby? If we continue to develop medical technologies that enable babies to live who are born after one or two months of gestation—especially those with physical or genetic difficulties—we are in effect saying that we are not going to stop until every time a spermatozoa fertilizes an ovum, "we" are going to "have" a child. Where can nature's rhythms of evolution take control? Even a cursory review of reproduction in nature shows that the potential is always there for overwhelming numbers of offspring, whether it be mosquitoes depositing larvae or an oak tree dropping acorns. So what should we do in human situations like that in which, as the Georgia newspaper article reported, "the child probably would have been retarded in any case?"

Much too briefly, I have raised two questions: (1) Should we continue to develop costly medical technologies that will be unavailable to masses of people? (2) Must we save every baby? It seems to me that the answers lie in our re-examining our use of technology. In response to the first question: at present, technology is basically for the privileged; in Christian terms, therefore, it should be judged immoral. Attempting to answer the second question, we should re-examine the nature of life and death to understand its joy and pains, but also to recognize the inevitability of some things that are beyond our control. In both situations it is clear that the poor are left out. Can you imagine newborn intensive care units being spread around the world? And can you imagine the cost? If you can, you can readily conclude that it will not happen—there are too many poor for the present high-cost system of medical technology. Imagine, on the other hand, that we found ways to share medical technology and knowledge without tying them to the economics of wealth.

A technology of sufficiency—or manna

What is needed is a technology of sufficiency, a technology that recognizes not only the need for ecological balance but also for human balance. Look, for example, at the difference between nuclear and solar technologies. Ecologically, the important question is that while one creates tons of highly-poisonous radioactive wastes that have to be looked after for tens of thousands of years, the other has no deadly by-product. In terms of human balance: why develop machines that require agriculture to be carried out by systems of huge mechanized monocropping when the overriding purposes of agriculture are to keep us in touch with living nature and to bring forth food? Why develop technologies that separate us from a healthy balanced life?

Let me try to stretch our thinking with a mixed metaphor: the technology of manna. I am intrigued by the connection between the idea of a technology of manna and a technology of sufficiency. In a technology of sufficiency, what is most important is the presence of "enough". It meets basic needs, not stimulated consumerism. This is crucial, because just as we can pollute our environmental systems to the point of breakdown, so we can push human systems to the point of breakdown through massive technologically-based consumerism. For example, the more nuclear weapons we produce in the quest for security, the less secure we become because of the increased odds of their being used by virtue of their sheer number!

By "technology of manna" I am thinking of a technological mindset based on the principle of "enough", of sufficiency. As the Book of Exodus records it, in the wilderness God and the Israelites were involved in a constant struggle for control. Early on, indeed, "on the fifteenth day of the second month after they had left Egypt," the Israelites were having serious second thoughts about their choice. They complained to Moses and Aaron:

> We wish that the Lord had killed us in Egypt. There we could at least sit down and eat meat and as much other food as we wanted. But you have brought us out into this desert to starve us all to death.[6]

Can we not hear the same kind of lament from the poor in a technological world? They are being starved to death by being cut off from the technological world. Keep in mind I am not arguing that they are cut off because they do not receive the benefits of technology; I am saying that we are choosing the wrong technologies; indeed, we have developed a technological way of life that requires the poor.

So God heard the Israelites' complaints and arranged for a new food to appear each morning. After the dew evaporated from the desert a thin, flaky substance was left; it tasted like thin cakes made with honey. But there was a catch: each person was told to gather as much as he or she needed. Though some gathered more and some less than the prescribed two quarts for each member of a household, "When they measured it, those who gathered too much did not have too much, and those who gathered less did not have too little."[7] They were also instructed not to save any for the next day, but as can be expected from people, some did hoard it. Lo and behold, the next day it "was full of worms and smelled rotten."

From this story we can ponder the present situation of both technology and of the poor. Why do we need to develop huge, costly, complex technological systems to do simple things like providing for energy and food? Why can we not have a technological way that produces what we need without requiring overconsumption and overdevelopment?

The Apostle Paul alluded to the importance of this kind of attitude in 2 Corinthians 8:13-14:

> I am not trying to relieve others by putting a burden on you; but since you have plenty at this time, it is only fair that you should help those who are in need. Then, when you are in need and they have plenty, they will help you. In this way both are treated equally

Instead of changing the poor, change the technology

Can we take technology and the Bible seriously at the same time? Not that technological ways and Biblical ways are going to replace each other—but we might recognize the fact that they have an essential complimentarity. William Stringfellow has written on this in terms of resistance to technology:

> For Biblical people, the claim goes further: Technology and technical capability must be rendered accountable to human life and to the sovereignity of the Word of God, in whom all things, including science and technology, and all of life, including that of the principalities and nations, have been created.[8]

Stringfellow argues that Christians have a responsibility to speak against the development of technologies aimed to destroy life, such as nuclear weapons—a responsibility based on "their confession that Jesus Christ is Lord."

Can the poor people get a robot too? According to our present technological attitudes the answer is no. Simply, no. Indeed, the poor are the human robots that make the mechanical ones possible.

A friend reminded me recently that being poor is not a simple thing. It is a network of difficulties that surrounds and entraps. Escape it is not simply a matter of desire. Wishing will not change the rules of a system based on technological progress. For who makes the rules? Why is it that the anchovies Peruvians fish from the ocean go to feed livestock and poultry in rich countries while those who fish remain poor? Why is it that a European government will give an East African country the gift of a textile factory so highly automated it needs only five hundred workers? And place the factory in a rural area where there is much unemployment? We need to challenge the basic assumption that the poor need to become as industrialized as we are. What would happen if instead of trying to change the poor, we changed the technology?

The temptation in this essay is to move toward an overpowering analysis of the terrible condition of the poor, their numbers, the bleakness of their life, their lack of food and shelter. But such an analysis is already available from all sides. The facts have been gathered; the pictures of swollen bellies have been published. Let us instead explore what it means. Let us accept the fact that our present approach toward the poor is basically one of crumbs falling from the tables of the rich. What we must realize is two-fold: that there are not enough crumbs falling, and that the crumbs that do fall worsen their lot. For instance, the tragedy of Bhopal, India illustrates the results of unsafe technological practices in one poor area. But chemical pollution is a daily presence in the settlements of the poor across the globe.

To look in a different direction we need to shake ourselves in two ways: first, we must reassess the kind of technology we are using and developing; second, we must experience anew the situation of the poor. There is a basic fact of industrialized life that Jim Wallis has expressed this way: "Our overconsumption is theft from the poor."[9] The problem is, we do not have any experience of those whom we steal from; thus we cannot even begin to understand how our technology must change.

Not only is our experience of the poor absent or inconsequential, the usual attitude is that it is the task or duty of the *poor* to change — to become like us. Ponder, however, the following litany written by a Two-Thirds World bishop and quoted by Henri Nouwen in *¡Gracias!*

WALK WITH US IN OUR SEARCH

Help us discover our own riches; don't judge us poor because we lack what you have.
Help us discover our chains; don't judge us slaves by the type of shackles you wear.

Be patient with us as a people; don't judge us backward simply because we don't follow your stride.
Be patient with our pace; don't judge us lazy simply because we can't follow your tempo.
Be patient with our symbols; don't judge us ignorant because we can't read your signs.
Be with us and proclaim the riches of your life which you can share with us.
Be with us and be open to what we can give.
Be with us as a companion who walks with us—neither behind nor in front—in our search for life and ultimately for God![10]

What is obvious but not always appreciated is the fact that the poor are real. As E. F. Schumacher put it: "They are actual people, as real as you and I, except that they can do things which you and I can't do."[11] He goes on to point out that you can calculate that somewhere around half a million people on the planet survive on less than fifty dollars each a year. The fact is, they do survive. They survive in an environment and in a way that we, the affluent, would not like, but they survive—they have the "know-how". If we approach them as poor souls who are lucky that we came along with our technological way, then we are, in effect, saying that what they know for survival does not count! In his last public speech before his death, Schumacher had this to say:

When I had asked myself this question, 'What would be the appropriate technology for rural India or rural Latin America or maybe the city slums?' I came to a very simple provisional answer. That technology would indeed be really much more intelligent, efficient, scientific if you like, than the very low level technology employed there, which kept them very poor. But it should be very, very much simpler, very much cheaper, very much easier to maintain, than the highly sophisticated technology of the modern West. In other words, it would be an intermediate technology, somewhere in between.[12]

Workers in the vineyard

Can the poor people have a robot too? That is the wrong question. It is not a matter of bringing them "up" to our standards. It is a matter of our accepting and bringing them into the "game" as co-creatures of God. In the parable of the workers in the vineyard (Matthew 20), some workers were hired in the morning and some at the last hour of the day. When it came time to pay them, the last ones hired lined up first. When they were paid the same wage that the all-day workers had agreed to, the expectations of the latter grew. But alas, they were paid the same. When they grumbled, the owner of the vineyard told them, "Now take your pay and go home. I want to give this laborer who was hired last as much as I gave you. Don't I have the right to do as I wish with my own money? Or are you jealous because I am generous?"

I have always tried to puzzle out the meaning of this parable as if it were directed from the rich to the poor. I could accept the generosity, but not the unfairness. However, when I turned it around once and saw it as directed from the poor to the rich, a different meaning emerged. However the rich define things, whether as fairness or as generosity, they do not allow for the full human participation of the poor—those who worked only the last hour of the day. Seen this way, Jesus' concluding comment: "so those who are last will be first, and those who are first will be last," turns the table on ordinary ways, which are now seen as exploitative. Thus it is with our technology. The knowledge "fuel" that is required for the growth of consumerism and consumption feeds on the lives of those at the bottom. What we need is a technology that meets the needs of all the people, those who work all day, as well as the last hour, a technology that is not geared only to the needs of exploitative growth.

In conclusion, we must recognize that the technologies we use are selected and developed out of political and economic considerations. They are not neutral. And if our political and economic systems are oriented against the poor, so also will be the technologies they use. From Kirkpatrick Sale:

> The particular technological variation that becomes developed is always the one that goes to support the various keepers of power. Hence in an age of high authoritarianism and bureaucratic control in both governmental and corporate realms, the dominant technology tends to reinforce those characteristics—ours is not an age of the assembly line and the nuclear plant by accident.[13]

As Gandhi put it in an oft-quoted formula: "The poor of the world cannot be helped by mass production, only by production of the masses."[14]

Our present technological road has no robots for the poor.

EIGHT

INVENTING THE FUTURE

Andy was getting ready to leave. A boy who had grown up on a Kentucky farm, he was turning toward manhood in a strange city with new books and voices. He was headed to college from his last summer on the farm. As Wendell Berry wrote about him: "now there lay in him a strange sorrow that seemed not to go away even when he was thoughtless of it or asleep".[1] But when Andy put his mind to it, he knew what it was: "it was the fear that in order to be what he might become he would have to cease to be what he had been."[2]

Yes, Andy, the future is as much a ceasing of something as it is a beginning of something. Indeed, one of the greatest inhibiting forces about the future is our inability to give some things up. Sometimes we put this down to "what difference will it make?" We say, "I fix leaky faucets, but my neighbors water their lawns all night, so my contribution toward conservation is just an insignificant drop in the bucket." Or we hear a woman say, "I take the Pill but I know five other women who won't or don't, so how will I help the population problem?" The difference is in what we ourselves become when we give up old ways in our search for a better world.

Technologies that die so others will grow

One important parameter of inventing the future is to understand the nature of balance and of growth. We have been enamored of material change and have put a high premium on new gadgets.

Things like digital clocks in ballpoint pens, electronic scales that you can read without bending over, electric knives, toothbrushes and pencil sharpeners, around-the-clock banking machines. The list goes on and on. My point is not simply to ridicule gadgets but to focus attention on our way of seeing change as material progress, as a better machine. For James Robertson, however, the future should not be seen as continuing expansion, but as balance: "balance within ourselves, balance between ourselves and other people, balance between people and nature."[3]

Future expansion, he believes, should be psychological and social in nature as we strive to "give top priority to learning to live supportively with one another on a small and crowded planet." The aim of invention should not be to create continuously new models of gadgets; rather, it should be to seek new ways of organizing ourselves into communities to help people fulfill themselves as individuals and members of the community. Then we will have achieved a future significantly different from the one now projected, oriented around the production of material goods. To be sure, material goods will be needed in greater quantity as more and more people share in improvements to their physical lives. But the production of digital clock ballpoint pens may drop to such a low priority as to disappear. The essence of balance is to ask which is more important: intellectual and economic activity required to feed people, for instance, or to make fancy disposable pens.

Balance is also evidenced through our expectations for growth. James Robertson uses an analogy with patterns of growth in trees.

> For example, as the new shoots and twigs of a tree take over the process of growth from the old wood, growth ceases in the trunk and main branches. Are the over-developed industrial countries like trees in which the old wood of economic activity is hardening and reaching the limits of its growth, while the buds of psychological and social development are forming the new shoots of growth? If the tree were a rose tree or a fruit tree, we would prune it—to get new growth in the right places. Is there an equivalent way of pruning old growth in the social and human sphere?[4]

Robertson also uses a biological analogy in depicting the balances of growth and death.

> All plants and creatures have a natural life cycle—birth, growth, maturity, decline and death. Do we forget this in our attempts to prolong life, not only for individual people but also for organ-

izations and institutions? Finally, the existence of each plant or creature to some extent enables and to some extent prevents the growth of others; and by its eventual death, it may create conditions in which others may grow. Do we tend to forget that, as individuals and as part of the institutions to which we belong, we can create conditions for others to grow in, not only by growing ourselves but also by declining? Is this what Christians mean when they say that Christ died that we may live?[5]

If inventing a future means we will deal seriously with "pruning old growth" and creating "conditions in which others may grow," we will certainly be inventing a different future than one of technological progress that is so uni-dimensional with respect to material goods. Can we imagine technologies that would die so that other technologies may live? Imagine star wars missile technology disappearing and a bake sale having to be held to raise money for the military. Imagine agriculture where people grew food for themselves, not for export. Imagine economic investment in self-sufficient craft materials instead of supersonic jets. Imagine inventing a future that puts a higher value on social growth than on economic growth, on the quality of life than on Gross National Product.

When to say no

In Frank Herbert's *Children of Dune,* Leto says to Stilgar, "The past may show the right way to behave if you live in the past, Stil, but circumstances change."[6] Yes, circumstances change. What madness it would be to suppose that we could change the material face of our lives without changing our spiritual values. Why should we expect to send young men and women out of rural lives into urban educations and think that their ties with nature will not change? What madness is it to think that we can accelerate into a world of genetic engineering, nuclear missiles, computers and space flight and keep the same political alignments and assumptions?

Circumstances are changing, radically changing. But this does not mean that we should ignore the past and do everything on the cutting edge of "trying-it-out." What is needed is neither an analysis of how it went in the past or might go in the future, but the growth of a passion for quality, for wholeness, for love and for realizing how what we do affects those who are "left out". To use an old-fashioned word, what we need is "gumption". As Robert Pirsig expressed it in *Zen and the Art of Motorcycle Maintenance:*

My personal feeling is that this is how any further improvement of the world will be done: by individuals making Quality decisions and that's all. God, I don't want to have any more enthusiasm for big programs full of social planning for big masses of people that leave individual Quality out. These can be left alone for a while. There's a place for them but they've got to be built on a foundation of Quality within the individuals involved. We've had that individual Quality in the past, exploited it as a natural resource without knowing it, and now it's just about depleted. Everyone's just about out of gumption.[7]

Yes, "a return to individual integrity, self-reliance and old-fashioned gumption." What we seem to have forgotten is how to say no. We rush ahead in our eagerness and forget that one aspect of Quality is to say no. By this I do not mean a rejection of the technological way, for I agree with Pirsig that a "hatred of technology is self-defeating."

The Buddha, the Godhead, resides quite as comfortably in the circuits of a digital computer or the gears of a cycle transmission as he does at the top of a mountain or in the petals of a flower. To think otherwise is to demean the Buddha—which is to demean oneself.[8]

A story by Loren Eiseley sets the dilemma in poetic but sharp focus.

The tragedy of a single man in the New York blackout in 1965 could easily become the symbol for an entire civilization. This man, as it happened, was trapped by the darkness on an upper floor of a skyscraper. A Negrito or any one of the bush folk would have known better than to go prowling in a spirit-haunted, leopard-infested jungle after nightfall. The forest dwellers would have remained in their huts until daybreak.

In this case civilized man was troubled by no such inhibitions. Seizing a candle from a desk in his office, he made his way out into the corridor. Since the elevators were not running, he cast about for a stairway. Sighting what in the candlelight appeared to be a small service doorway near the bank of elevators, he opened it and, holding his small candle at eye level, stepped in. He was found the next day at the bottom of an elevator shaft, the extinguished candle still clutched in his hand.
I have said that this episode is symbolic. Man, frail, anticipatory man, no longer possessed the caution to find his way through a

I have said that this episode is symbolic. Man, frail, anticipatory man, no longer possessed the caution to find his way through a disturbance in his nightly routine. Instead he had seized a candle, the little flickering light of human knowledge, with which to confront one of his own giant creations in the dark. A janitor had left a door unlocked that should have been secured. Urban man, used to walking on smooth surfaces, had never glanced below his feet. He and his inadequate candle had plunged recklessly forward and been swallowed up as neatly by a machine in its tunnel as by a leopard on a dark path.[9]

Elevator shafts are creations of technology; leopards are creations of nature. To ignore either is to put ourselves at their mercy. The choice is not one between progress and stagnation, or between growth and no-growth. E. F. Schumacher challenged us:

> ... there is no single answer. For his present purposes man needs many different structures, both small ones and large ones, some exclusive and some comprehensive. Yet people find it most difficult to keep two seemingly opposite necessities of truth in their minds at the same time. They always tend to clamour for a final solution, as if in actual life there could be ever a final solution other than death.[10]

It all depends on what we are trying to do. What is the direction of balance? Of harmony? Of the appropriateness of a technology to our needs? To follow knowledge, we must serve *needs*. Thus to invent the future we must discover what we need.

God between the carnival and the computer

To get at needs we must pursue our perceptions as well as the facts. "How we see the future has everything to do with how we live in the present," is the way Hawken, Ogilvy, and Schwartz put it in their book *Seven Tomorrows.*[11] In response to the question, "Then how do you change?" John Naisbitt, in *Megatrends,* answered: "I would argue that you can't change *unless* you completely rethink what it is you are doing, unless you have a wholly new vision of what you are doing."[12]

In our adherence to the technological notion of progress, to use Theodore Roszak's delightful image: "We have trapped God somewhere between the brain physiologist's computer and the carnival funhouse where everything novel and naughty draws the crowd."[13] We have turned the presence of God in our industrialized world into the technological myth that "someday our prince will come." Someday technology will pop up with the answers and we will all live happily ever after.

Or to put it another way, consider a story told by Ivan Illich about a Mexican village he knew

> through which not more than a dozen cars drive each day. A Mexican was playing dominoes on the new hard-surface road in front of his house—where he had probably played and sat since his youth. A car sped through and killed him. The tourist who reported the event to me was deeply upset, and yet he said: "The man had it coming to him."[14]

The death of the Mexican was to be blamed on his idiocy for sitting on a hard-surface road built for cars. We accept unthinkingly the logic that technology does as it will and we must bend to it. To help see why this is so, Illich compares this incident to one in which a primitive Bushman reported the death of a friend by saying his friend had collided with a taboo and therefore had died. For the Bushman, unfortunate death had to be described in terms of the laws of magic so that the primitive himself would not have to bear any responsibility. For the tourist, the death of the Mexican was described in terms of the laws of mechanics; any person should know better than to get in the way of a speeding automobile. In neither case was there any responsibility for the death. The Bushman blamed it on "some tremendous and dumb transcendence" and the tourist on the "laws of science."

The tourist was in awe of the inexorable logic of the machine. The highway belonged to cars, not to people, even the road in front of someone's house. The responsibility of the one operating the car—the technology—was not brought into play. Thus the logic: technology does as it will and we must bend to it. We must change our lives to fit the needs of the road, is the tourist's message. And is this not the same kind of mindset we place ourselves in with regard to technology? We are caught between giving in to the presence of the computers and missiles (Isn't it grand how we can build bombs to win peace?) and the carnival (Isn't it grand how microwave ovens help the affluent cook faster?). We thus manage to disregard our responsibility for the impact of our technology. What is our response to the Mexican playing dominoes who gets wiped out by the "technological need" of someone else to get quickly from one place to another? We all too often leave God out of the picture—squeezed out between our inventions and our pleasure.

The test of technology is what happens to the poor

Is it possible for us to outpace our human wisdom? We have literally wired the planet with nuclear weapons on a six-minute timer and we hope that the collective wisdom will be found to prohibit unleashing them. We have literally inundated the industrialized countries (and increasingly the Two-Thirds World) with laboratory-created chemicals called drugs that keep people with serious defects alive long enough to allow them to reproduce and thus keep the "defective genes" in the human gene pool. And we hope that the collective wisdom will be found to keep this potential deterioration of the gene pool from being a major catastrophe. We have literally polluted the atmosphere with so much of an overload of sulfur chemicals that we must label certain rainfall as "acid rain". And we hope that we will eventually find the wisdom to counteract this global hazard that is sterilizing lakes and forests.

We are among the first generations of humans who are answering literally some of the kinds of questions God posed to Job. The Lord spoke to Job out of the storm: "Who are you to question my wisdom with your ignorant, empty words?" But how many of the following questions have we answered or are about to?

> Have you been to the springs in the depths of the sea?
> Have you walked on the floor of the ocean?
> Who dug a channel for the pouring rain . . . ?
> Do you know the laws that govern the skies, and can you make
>   them apply to the earth?
> Can you shout orders to the clouds and make them drench you
>   with rain?
> Was it you, Job, who made horses so strong . . . ?[15]

The Lord asked Job to "Stand up now like a man, and answer my questions . . ." Through our technological prowess we are doing just that: answering those questions and then some. We have become creators in our own right: creators of new species of life, of instantaneous global communication systems, of vehicles that travel through space, of computer memory banks that can store with instant access more information than we could ever remember even if all our efforts were given to memorization. Indeed, we may be on the verge of creating machines that by popular consent will be called "thinking" machines.

The questions I want to ask are not "Have we gone too far? Are we wrong to try to out-create the Creator?" No, the question I want to ask is one of *why? "Why* are we creating?" In Isaiah there are many passages about God's creation and promises; Isaiah 42:5 makes my point:

> God created the heavens and stretched them out;
> he fashioned the earth and all that lives there;
> he gave life and breath to all its people.

But why? That comes in the next verse: "I, the LORD, have called you and given you power to see that justice is done on earth."

It cannot be any clearer. We do have power. We are intelligent creatures. But we are also creatures in relationship, and in that relationship God calls us "to see that justice is done on earth." It cannot be any simpler. *The technology we choose must be a technology that does justice.* We cannot apply only the measurements of economics and science, we must also apply the political, social and psychological measurements of justice. And in the overall context of the biblical story, this means that we cannot ignore the poor.

We are told in Isaiah 42:7, "You will open the eyes of the blind and set free those who sit in dark prisons." It is easy enough to see how technology can help in the first instance: to help the blind see. What we must now learn to "see" is how technology can free the imprisoned, those whom certain technologies oppress and keep in bondage. By rewarding large landowners in Two-Thirds World countries who use high-tech agricultural methods, we allow hundreds of thousands of peasants to remain poor and unable to benefit from their toil beyond creating a subsistence existence for themselves. By using nuclear technologies we not only put the entire globe in jeopardy from bombs of outrageous size and effect, we also demand that there be centralized institutions of power and knowledge that push economic costs almost beyond sight.

Our responsibility is "to see that justice is done on earth," and we need to learn how that applies to our use of technology. "For years," wrote theologian Richard Schaull, "we harbored the illusion that our advanced technological society would be able to produce enough to overcome poverty and point the way toward a solution for the Third World as well."[16] Increasingly, however, we are seeing that the goods we produce tend more to be consumer items like digital watches and video games. These do not change the lives of the poor, but serve to secure the gap between the rich and the poor. People in industrialized countries tend either to romanticize the fate of the poor ("Isn't it terrible, but things will get better") or blame them ("If only they would go out and get a decent job"). Schaull hit the target when he recalled that:

> . . . no part of our tradition has a more central place in our history than the Bible, and yet, for those of us who are white, middle-class Christians in the First World, the biblical story stands in the sharpest contrast to our own.[17]

Those of us who are not poor (that is, those reading this book) will not be able to hear the poor unless in some significant way we enter into their world.

Schaull summed up the writings of contemporary Latin American theologians by saying that they have uncovered a central theme in the prophetic writings: "To know God is to practice justice to the poor."[18]

> In other words, *the test of justice is what happens to the poor,* to those who have nothing, are powerless, and have no one to defend them.[19]

Though it may sound strange at first, it is necessary to say that the *test of technology* is what happens to the poor. We have kept technology separate as an idea, thinking of it as science's magical tool to deliver the goods and somehow create a better world. It is time we brought technology into the whole picture, along with our values, our political processes, our social realities and our religious consciousness. High tech agriculture oppresses the poor. It does not improve their lot. Nuclear technologies oppress the poor. They divert incredible economic and human resources toward a supposed deterrence of war. Or toward a supposed need for having enough electricity to be able to use chain saws to cut butter. Some agricultural technologies do improve the lot of the small farmer but these are not spread, for the pressure of progress demands sophisticated, costly technologies. Some energy technologies use the sun's energy and do not require huge, sophisticated, costly power plants. To shift economic and human resources toward helping the poor help themselves would be a revolution of unprecedented magnitude. What we have to realize was expressed by Jacques Ellul:

> What it comes to is that technology increases the technician's freedom, i.e., his power, his control. And the so-called freedom due to technology always boils down to that growth of power.[20]

It is time that we use technology for the growth of the power of the poor. If we take seriously Isaiah's words of the Lord God to us, as servants, "to see that justice is done on earth," we are going to have to answer the question: Whose side are we on?

Don't take my dreams away

But there is also the reality of dreams. What is often so hard for those of us in the industrialized world to understand is that our dreams are not the same as those of most of the people on this planet. To invent the future we are going to have to begin sharing some new stories—to find a new "dreaming reality". In the following story about a slum dweller in Chile, told by Ariel Dorfman, a Chilean writer, we can get a glimpse of the differences:

> I didn't notice anything special about her. Misery has a way of leveling individual nuances . . . She was very poor, and lived in one of the numerous shantytowns that mushroom around all big cities in Latin America. They brim with migrant workers and their families. She, like them, had built a small shack out of any stray sort of material that life had washed within her reach. I vaguely recall that she had children, and there must have been many of them. The rest is conjecture, almost a sociological construct, valid for her as for so many other women living in those subhuman conditions. Filth, disease, hunger, and a husband who was unemployed, alcoholic, or plagued by worse demons.[21]

As it turned out, this woman had heard that Dorfman was on a crusade against comics, soap operas, radio and TV sitcoms, which he believed to be imports into Chilean culture with no redeeming qualities. He was in the woman's area as a volunteer helping to clean up the destruction after a violent thunderstorm when she came up to him and asked him if he was the one who thought people shouldn't read photo novels (romantic love stories told through photographs of handsome actors and actresses). Dorfman stopped working and said that yes, it was true. He told her that "photo novels were a hazard to her health and her future." She replied in a familiar, tender tone: "Don't do that to us, *compañerito*. Don't take my dreams away from me."[22]

The woman wanted to dream, but Dorfman wanted to dissect those dreams and expose them as models of oppression. To Dorfman, the dreams were imported.

> I believed that these models and illustrations clashed head-on with the immediate needs of their consumers. This was especially so in a land like Chile, which imported most of these forms of entertainment or simply imitated them in bastardized local versions. We imported our weapons, our machinery, our banking techniques, our freeways, our technology. We also imported much of our popular culture.[23]

But the woman was not interested in this. She was interested in the value of the illusions that helped her survive. She was interested in making up for what was missing in her life, never mind if she was manipulated in the process.

A few months after Dorfman's encounter with the woman, Chile elected a new president, Salvador Allende. Over the next few years things changed dramatically. Allende's government nationalized Chile's resources and redistributed the land to those who tilled it. Workers began to participate in the management of the factories where they worked. The result was a shift toward democratizing Chile's institutions. By chance, Dorfman happened to run into the woman again. He did not recognize her, but she went up to him and announced that he was right and that she did not read "trash" like photo novels anymore. She said, "Now, *compañero*, we are dreaming reality."[24]

The radical change in Chile toward allowing the people a chance to have a say in their personal affairs had "awakened" the slum-dwelling woman. She no longer perceived those photo novels as real or natural. She had grown out of her old self that did not want dreams taken away from her, to a new self that was "dreaming reality."

For those of you who know Chile, you know that her dreaming reality did not last. Allende was overthrown with the help of American CIA involvement. The woman, and tens of thousands like her, again came into the presence of nightmares that knew only the burning reality of oppression. How can we in the industrialized world understand the kind of reality of a woman who one day could say that "she was tired of living on trash," and another day heard "the sound of military boots in her neighborhood and realized that she was no longer allowed to think — let alone live or work — for herself."

Trends will not invent the future

One of the many books on the future on my shelves, *Encounter with the Future: A Forecast of Life into the 21st Century* by Marvin Cetron and Thomas O'Toole, illustrates a serious problem we have with trends. The book is a collection of short scenarios covering a wide range of topics. Among them: Women Rabbis; Sweden, the Bellwether Nation; New Drugs for Pain; Heavy Oil; China is Leapfrogging; and Tax Bracket Creep. It is interesting reading in a way, a kind of playing with what might happen. But as a book of "encounter with the future" it is not only a dismal failure, but grossly misleading with a mind-boggling hedging of all possibilities. To illustrate:

> Look for much of the world to suffer water shortages but look for much of the world to solve its water shortages.[25]

> We'll feel better, we'll look better, and we'll live longer. Of course, there will be change but it won't be the kind of change that worsens our lot in life. There will be hardship but most of it will be the kind of hardship we can endure and overcome.[26]

> [And to conclude the book, this jewel:]
> The years ahead may be difficult, but on the whole they are years of hope and promise.[27]

Cetron and O'Toole's problem is they would not cope with the moral or image aspects of the future. They defend themselves from such a charge by writing:

> In this book we make no moral judgments. If we say that divorce is on the rise and that men and women may take as many as three wives and husbands during their lives we're not saying that because we'd like that to happen. We're saying it because the trends of the times are predicting it will happen.[28]

But trends will not invent the future. If we follow trends, we move backwards into the future without any image or dream of what could be.

What is more damaging, in my view, is that the authors deliberately avoid challenging the way things are. They blithely assume that the future is a trend projection, so they write: "Despite the problems and perils of the human condition, our book forecasts that most of the world's people will go right on improving their lot."[29] What follows is this:

> The blind will get technological help to see and the deaf to hear. Paraplegics will walk away from their wheelchairs as research begins to prove that spinal cord injuries are reparable . . . There will be medicines that cure phobias . . . we shall all be feeling better in the years ahead . . . The time is not far off when people will live as long as trees.[30]

Ah so, and the poor will continue to suck air and wonder if manna ever existed? Is that not a trend too? Where is the trend for Mary's song of praise in Luke 1? "He has filled the hungry with good things and sent the rich away with empty hands." Where is the trend — not for the promise of technologically-improved eyes for the blind, but for the proclamation "of liberty to the captives and recovery of sight to the blind? (Luke 4:18) That is the problem with futurists who forecast with technological clothes on. They cannot see that we create the future not only by continuing what is possible, but by doing what is now *not possible*.

The kind of "encounters" Cetron and O'Toole describe were exposed by Matthew, when he quoted from Isaiah (Matthew 13:14, 15a):

> This people will listen and listen, but not understand; they will look and look but not see, because their minds are dull, and they have stopped up their ears and have closed their eyes.

The problem with *Encounters with the Future* is that it fails to address anything but the technological trends of the present. The authors ignore their own advice from the opening sentence: "Time was when we grew up to do what our parents did, live where they lived, worship where they worshipped and think what they thought."[31] The writers say that that time is gone forever, but then they proceed to forecast trends and scenarios as if the future were unfolding as the same *kind* of time as that in which they grew up. That is not what we need — we need the unfolding of a future we want to live in, not one that trends will put us in. We need a time unfolding that takes into account a commitment to live as well as a commitment to technology.

Kurt Vonnegut, Jr. offers this serious advice: "We are what we pretend to be so we'd better be careful what we pretend."[32] That is the kind of "encounter" we need—with what we pretend to be, not with trends.

In the quiet recognition that the old won't do

What does it mean to "invent" the future? Invention is a technological word signifying the active use of human ability and imagination to "think up" a new machine that either solves some kind of problem or makes some new thing possible. Inventions are things to be patented, and though they may be widely used, they are personal or corporate property. What I want to do is start with this technological word and enlarge its meaning to include vision, expectation and the desire for justice. I want to use the word to embrace "yearning", that human quest for something "better". But not better because of the invention of a new machine. Better because of the discovery of a new way of being in relationship with God, others, self and nature. Better in the realization of dreams of quality, not goals of quantity.

Such invention is both a personal and a communal task. It begins with a recognition of the whole—the whole person or the whole community, be it village, city or the globe. It is based on a commitment to making choices out of this recognition. Such invention does not involve a formula or set of directions. It is by nature pluralistic and celebrates a rainbow of different cultures and views. What is asked of those who want to "invent the future" is a willingness to begin simply, to struggle to know how to replace the controlling values of greed and selfishness with values of sharing and love. Our technological lifestyle is like a gilded cage; those of us in the so-called developed world are inside. We must invent ways to see those outside our cage and, in seeing, realize that the gilded cage must go.

In a *New Yorker* cartoon, the King announces that he can so repair Humpty Dumpty—all he needs are more horses and more men! That attitude does not lead us to invention. It will not lead to new vision or to the struggle to see the "others" of our world. The king's mindset sees the answers to all questions as more of the same, more of the technology that built the gilded cage in the first place. More important, however, is the question: more of what? Should we put Humpty Dumpty together again? Will a desire to be faithful be served by more of our present "solutions", which lead to more pollution, more weapons, more poverty, more hunger — in a word, more injustice?

Marilyn Ferguson's startling image captures the starting place: "the invention we need comes out of the quiet recognition that the old won't do."[33]

> Of one thing I am certain: Life
> is not accompanied by inescapable
> certitudes but by visions, risks,
> and passions.
>
> — Rubem Alves

POSTSCRIPT: ARE WE DYING OR BEING BORN?

Are we dying or being born? Both. Biologically, each of us is aging, which sooner or later means death. Cultures, lifestyles and fads fade and pass into the corridors of memory. But something replaces them; something is born.

To consider that birth I turn to the compelling, haunting story of Riddley Walker. From the fertile imagination of Russell Hoban has sprung a story of multilayered imagery and challenge. At one level, it is the story of a young man at the time of his rite of passage. He lives in a post-holocaust age in which surviving humans have become separated into bands of tough, suspicious folk trying desperately to search out some undefined proof of meaning. Somehow, they believe, there is some thing or some knowledge somewhere that will grant incalculable rewards to the finder. So Riddley is plunged not only into the search for himself, but also into a search for survival, for a future. As he tells a friend:

> If you cud even jus see 1 thing clear the woal of whats in it you cud see everything clear. But you never will get to see the woal of any thing youre all ways in the middl of it living it or moving thru it.[1]

Another level comes from Hoban's creation ("invention") of a unique spelling that makes reading the book somewhat like reading in a foreign language. *Worl* for world. *Woal* for whole. *Qwyet* for quiet. *Sylents* for silence. Hoban's spelling produces another level of meaning—or better, a powerful way of experiencing the "riddles" of Riddley Walker's search, riddles that touch the spaces of soul rather than the stars of intellect. In Riddley's search there is a transcendence, a meta-layer of meaning above the story and plot that is intensified by the different spelling.

Riddley stops during one of his adventures to muse about what is happening to him. He senses that he is being driven by an urge to find something. This urge is leading him to behave in strange ways (e.g., he impulsively leaps a fence, leaving the security of his human band to follow instead a huge, dangerous, but compelling dog). But Riddley has no idea what he is seeking. His quest has no image or form. He knows only that the more he tries, the more things happen to him.

As he says:

> The worl is ful of things waiting to happen. Thats the meat and boan of it right there. You myt think you can jus go here and there doing nothing. Happening nothing. You cant tho you bleeding cant. You put your self on any road and some thing will show its self to you. Wanting to happen. Waiting to happen. You myt say, 'I dont want to know.' But 1ce its showt its self to you you will know wont you. You cant not know no mor. There it is and working in you. You myt try to put a farness be twean you and it only you cant becaws youre carrying it inside you. The waiting to happen aint out there where it ben no more its inside you.[2]

Once something is shown to you, you cannot ignore it. It works inside you. Once you start out on a road and get some experience, you become different. As long as you do not know or have not seen, what can you do? But once you have, how can you not do something?

Teilhard de Chardin expressed this same idea: "A truth once seen, even by a single mind, always ends by imposing itself on the totality of human consciousness."[3] And in *Dune Messiah,* Frank Herbert wrote about "lonely power":

> No matter how exotic human civilization becomes, no matter the developments of life and society nor the complexity of the machine/human interface, there always come interludes of lonely power when the course of humankind, the very future of humankind, depends upon the relatively simple actions of single individuals.[4]

The poignant, telling line of Riddley's search, and one that I embrace in this exploration of technology, values and faithfulness, comes when Riddley says:

May be the idea of it ben waiting all them years for me to come
a long and be it.[5]

Yes, maybe you are the one! You may not be Jonah or Moses or
Mary, but you are one who counts, whom God is calling. If the future
does not depend on *you* making a difference, then who is left?

May be the idea of it ben waiting all them years for me to come
a long and be it.

May be . . .

LEADER'S GUIDE

INTRODUCTION

SIMPLE ACTIONS OF SINGLE INDIVIDUALS

Let me begin with two quick stories. The first comes from the days of great general excitement about space travel. I remember a U.S. Senator exclaiming, "We are the masters of the universe. We can go anywhere we choose." When I heard that I was reminded of another thought: "If you don't know where you are going, any road will get you there."

The second story comes from E. F. Schumacher. Two monks, both smokers, were trying to settle the question of whether or not it was okay to smoke while praying. The monks finally decided to ask their respective abbots. One got into deep trouble for asking such a question, while the other got a response of encouragement. When they met to compare answers, the monk who had gotten into trouble wanted to know just what it was that the other monk had asked. The second monk replied, "I asked whether it was permissible to pray while smoking."

These two stories set the stage for a discussion of technology in tension with human values. On the one hand, we must be clear about where it is we want to go. On the other hand, we must recognize that while our inner senses know the profound differences between "praying while smoking" and "smoking while praying," it makes no difference at all to our outer senses.

We have become used to thinking about technology as something separate that stands by itself and provides us with endless change. But even though technology indeed changes our outer world, we must recognize that it also has a profound impact on our inner world. Technology is not only about technical things; it is also about spirit and values. We must consider what technology does to our inner selves.

How the sessions are structured

The eight sessions that follow are intended as a guide for group discussions. Each session begins with a set of assumptions about the specific topic being discussed. My intention is that the group start out by discussing the validity and implications of these assumptions. What do they agree on? Where are there disagreements? It is important to think hard about the implications of these assumptions since this is where our values and behavior come in. If the group challenges any of the assumptions, they should go on to discuss what other assumptions might replace them and what their likely implications would be. Five questions follow, drawn from both the essays and the assumptions. As the group answers the questions they should bring into play additional reading and personal experiences.

Each session concludes with three quotations. The first two are intended to be controversial enough to start a creative argument. The third quotation, from the Bible, helps us reflect on how we are to make sense of stories written in a time when technology was quite different from what it is today.

To begin the discussion, a variety of group discussion techniques can be used. The entire group might want to meet to talk over the assumptions, then divide up to consider the individual questions and quotations and come together again to report back. There are many other ways a discussion can be structured and leaders should feel free to adapt to their own situation.

Additional ideas and activities

A discussion of the essays in *The Speed of Love* and the material in the companion book, *21st Century Pioneering: A Scrapbook of the Future* can be supplemented by a variety of activities, for instance:

Visits To Make

1. Plan a visit to a hospital or television station. Get permission to be shown as much equipment as possible. Ask questions about how the equipment works. Ask about the impact of its use on people. Ask what new equipment is expected in the future and what it might do.

2. Visit a night shelter or soup kitchen enough times to be comfortable in the setting. Talk with people there about their views on technology.

3. Look around your neighborhood or city for signs that solar energy is being used—for instance, collectors on a rooftop or in a backyard. Ask the person(s) who live there to talk about their experience with solar energy. The same thing can be done for windmills, methane generators and a nuclear power plant.

4. If you have never done so before, ask a friend to go with you to visit a computer sales store. Get an idea of the range of computers available.

Things to Do

1. Collect newspaper or magazine clippings about any technology. Make a list of comments they make: what is good about technology? What do they say is bad? Then determine what values are evident in these clippings.

2. Prepare a list of computer jargon words and make up a story using them. Read it to others to stimulate conversation. (e.g., programmed, hacker, on-line, log in, hardwired, software, buffer, default, debug.)

3. Try to find out what credit check companies have in their files about you. In other words, check into how technology has an impact on your privacy. For starters, you can ask a lawyer, a business person or a banker about how to find out.

4. Television and movies are good sources for technological ideas yet to come. Select an example and make a list of the values that would be needed to support that technology, e.g., Michael Knight's car KITT, Star Wars movies.

People to Invite

In each of the suggestions that follow, the idea is to listen to a human story and then ponder its implications for the tension between technology and values. Some stories might be positive, others negative. It is important to hear each person's story with sensitivity and respect. Those who share their stories may be members of the discussion group or people invited from outside the group.

1. Gather an intergenerational group to share reminiscences about the introduction of new technologies. For starters: the zipper (1913), frozen foods (1923), hybrid corn (1933), nylon (1939), antibiotics (1940), the ballpoint pen (1945), Hiroshima (1945), automatic car transmissions (1946), television (1947), long-playing records (1948), kidney transplants (1954), instant coffee (1955), the Salk polio vaccine (1955), oral contraceptives (1960), Neil Armstrong on the moon (1969). What others can you think of?

2. Put together a panel of persons over fifty and under twenty. Have the older persons talk about the technologies they grew up with before age twenty. Then ask the younger persons to talk about what technologies they expect to see when they are over fifty.

3. See if you can find someone who lost a job because a machine took over and is willing to talk about the experience.

4. Ask someone working in the airline travel business to talk about the use of computers in that industry.

5. Ask some young people who are studying computers in school to talk about how they use the computer and what they think the future of computers might be.

6. Ask someone who once purchased a computer but no longer uses it to share what happened.

7. If possible, have the discussion group meet in the presence of a computer with someone demonstrating what it can do.

8. Ask someone from a medical field to talk about changes in medical technology—e.g., a physician, a dentist, a nurse, a hospital administrator.

9. Ask an automobile mechanic to talk about changes in automobile technology.

10. Have someone bring in a TV video camera to demonstrate it and talk about its potential uses.

11. Ask someone who has a heart pacemaker, or is on kidney dialysis (or has been), or has had an organ transplant to talk about the technology that saved his or her life. If that person is willing, ask to what extent he or she would want a technology to continue his or her life.

12. Ask someone who is (or has been) in the military to talk about personal experiences with military technology—e.g., hand weapons, tanks, aircraft, ships, missile silos, research.

13. Ask someone with farming experience to talk about changes in agricultural technology—e.g., new machines, new seeds, economic and social impact.

14. Ask someone who was born and raised in a Two-Thirds World country to talk about technology in that country.

Two pleas in closing: First, recognize that there are far more ideas in each session than can be discussed in a one-hour gathering. Also, take into account that an hour-long discussion usually ends up less than that due to announcements, special sharing, people coming in late and leaving early, etc. The second plea is to recognize that it is quite easy to keep a discussion on the level of clichés which, in effect, close off the discovery of new insights. One example is the oft-expressed idea that "technology" and "science" are two different things—that science means gaining fundamental knowledge and doing basic research, while technology means the use of that knowledge—applied research. Though this idea has its validity, it does not help us explore the tension that exists between the use of technology and our values. Another example is the statement that technology is "neutral," and that it is how it is used that makes it good or bad. This is often followed by the illustration that the atomic bomb is "neutral" and it is only when it is used that it becomes bad or good. Again, that may be so—but only as far as it goes. The existence of atomic bombs requires a huge, centralized, military-industrial, political and economic society. A certain type of society means a certain type of behavior. Values are not isolated from the technology. Further, the presence of atomic bombs literally holds the world hostage because of their incredible destructive power. This is hardly a neutral matter. So in your discussion, probe deeper than statements that avoid the tension that can exist between technology and values.

I have found that people in trying to respond to hard questions about technology, often end up saying, "Well, that's it. The problem has been identified." Examples of how the problem is identified?

"Science will handle it" (wait for a technical fix);

"God will provide" (no effort on our part is needed);

"Let's get back to nature" (de-industrialization);

"I'm all right, Jack" (look after yourself, friend, I've got mine);

"We need triage" (we can only save those who are not hopeless);

"Scapegoat" (someone, something else is responsible);

"Doomsday is approaching" (Repent!).

The trouble is, labeling a problem usually ends the discussion! The answers I am hoping to stimulate through these discussions are in an important way not *answers,* but *commitments* to biblically-based values. In other words, answers that will have an impact on our behavior and enhance our biblical faithfulness. Try to help people move beyond simply labeling the problem. Help them move toward what they can *do* about the problem.

To sum up: We need to reconcile what we know in our heads with what we know in our hearts. Or to quote 1 John 3:18: "My children, our love should not be just words and talk; it must be true love, which shows itself in action."

A TRUTH NOT TO BE IGNORED

"No matter how exotic human civilization becomes, no matter the development of life and society nor the complexity of the machine/human interface, there always come interludes of lonely power when the course of humankind, the very future of humankind, depends upon the relatively simple actions of single individuals."

(From *Dune Messiah* by Frank Herbert)

TECHNOLOGICAL PROGRESS
AND RELIGIOUS CONSCIOUSNESS

ASSUMPTIONS

Would you change or add to any of the following?

1. *Progress and Technology*

Technology is a central factor in determining progress in industrialized countries. The rational, objective, pragmatic, scientific knowledge of what can be done serves as the fuel that drives the economic, social and political determinations of what is done. The development of technology has become an imperative: if it can be done, it must be done; if we can change, we must.

2. *Problems and Solutions*

Even though we recognize that certain technologies create serious problems, our belief in progress maintains that the solution lies in the development of a better technology. Concern for justice is not recognized as a technological concern except in the corollary existence of the "trickle down theory"—i.e., that the fruits of technology will spill over to enhance the lives of the poor.

3. *Nature*

The prevailing view in industrialized countries is that nature is a raw material to be used for technological progress. Though care must be taken not to overly disrupt ecological balances, the human right to use any non-living material as we desire is not questioned. This extends also into the area of living materials, for instance, raising chickens in cages only for the purpose of getting their eggs or meat. If technology can develop "super-chickens," that will be all to the good, says the prevailing idea of progress.

4. *Religious Consciousness*

The growing impact of the preceding assumptions about technology, progress, problems, solutions and nature is increasingly negative, not only toward the quality of life but also toward the very existence of life. Without reawakening our religious commitment and consciousness, significant disaster is imminent for humankind, as well as the planet.

QUESTIONS

1. Do you agree or disagree that our present view of progress is based too much on analytical, scientific, objective thought and should be changed to include things like intuitive wisdom, compassion and ecological awareness? Illustrate why you agree or disagree.

2. Do you see any relationship between technological progress and religious consciousness? If so, what is it? If not, why not?

3. What do you believe our biblical "instructions" are? How are we doing on them?

4. Does it make any sense to try to draw connections between our technological abilities and a theological sense of servanthood? Said another way, is there really any relationship between technology and justice?

5. Does it make any sense to think about a "sacred ecology" — a sense of progress in which there would be a significant connection between technology and religion?

QUOTATIONS

1. What are the differences between Herman Kahn's expectations of growth and those of George T. Lock Land, as expressed in the following two statements?

   Kahn:

   > The scenario presented, elaborated and tested in this book can be summarized with the general statement that 200 years ago almost everywhere human beings were comparatively few, poor and at the mercy of the forces of nature, and 200 years from now, we expect, almost everywhere they will be numerous, rich and in control of the forces of nature .... [we will soon see that] the task of producing the necessities of life has become trivially easy because of technological advancement and economic development. We expect that all countries eventually will develop the characteristics of super and post-industrial societies .... assertions that an impending dramatic collision with physical limits will force a choice between a policy leading inevitably to catastrophe and one of no-growth (or even a forced low-growth) are, in our view, based on highly implausible assumptions.[1]

   Lock Land:

   > Growth is, after all, an irreversible phenomenon, and undeniable. As we study our planet and ecosystem, we find that Nature has never been content to settle for merely the successful. History, in every sense, from the biological to the social, demonstrates that what we really have to fear is not so much the perpetuation of our growth failures; much more dangerous is the deliberate attempt to repeat our successes. Today's successes become tomorrow's failures. The idea of "limiting growth" is anathema to Nature and to Man. Not only that, but just to "balance" growth would deny the very influences that created the ascending and achieved values and ideas most vital to our species. Life in its very manifestation is growth and change. Not to grow is to die.[2]

2. What do you think of Samuel Florman's view of placing the blame on technology, as expressed in the following statements?

Will, or life-force, or human nature—call it whatever you like—is what is at the root of our problems. Technology is merely one expression of this force. It is illogical to place the blame on technology. Why not blame the impulse to seek beauty, which we call art, or the impulse to seek truth, which we call philosophy, or the impulse to seek the ineffable "all," which we call religion? These are the sources of man's dreams and desires. These are the urges that drive man ever onward and refuse to let him rest. Man's technological skills may be responsible for the invention of the automobile, but he wants it and uses it because of his craving for new experiences, experiences of which he can conceive only because of his highly developed aesthetic sense and existential yearnings.

Further, if we are considering the source of man's discontent, let us remember that it is art, philosophy and religion that have made promises that cannot be kept. Technology's promises can be fulfilled. Visions of beauty, truth, and eternal bliss can only be mirages. Therefore, added to our real problems are the frustrations that must follow when we recognize that our dreams of Paradise can never be realized.[3]

3. Read Exodus 4:1–17. As you reflect on the story of God giving Moses miraculous power, think about the kinds of technological power humankind has today and what "miracles" God might be asking of *us*.

* * *

See Scrapbook, pages 2, 3, 8, 9, 12, 22, 34, 35 and 57 for additional discussion material.

SESSION TWO

VALUES AND SCALE

ASSUMPTIONS

Would you change or add to any of the following?

1. *Values*

    The prevailing values position in industrialized countries is that technology is neutral. That, however, is not so. The values of technology are different from those of human communities, which include compassion and love and from those of nature, which includes the natural cessation of growth.

2. *Scale*

    Technological progress is fueled by the assumption that bigger is better, or more is better; but scale is a matter of balance, not giantism or centralization.

3. *Alternative Technology*

    What is needed is a shift toward alternative technologies that spring from the human scale; that is, technologies rooted in local circumstances and having local, not global impact.

QUESTIONS

1. What, to you, are values? Give examples.

2. Do you associate any particular values with technology or do you believe that technology is neutral? If you do associate technology with values, which ones? If not, why not?

3. With regard to the growth of population and pollution, which of the following views do you hold?

   (a) the problems are being solved
   (b) we still face grave future danger

4. Should we shift from hard to soft technology? Why or why not?

5. How would you describe a technology on a human scale? What values would undergird it?

QUOTATIONS

1. Technology continues to change the ways we live and think. If Rubem Alves is right that we cannot go back to previous values, what values are we going toward? As he puts it:

   > We cannot preserve rural values in a technocratic world. Once upon a time peasants could resolve the problem of anomie that arose when they moved to the big city by going back to their original world. Today, however, the problem is no longer a spatial one. Something has happened to our space. It has been engulfed by the new time that bureaucratic and technological society has created. We cannot win out over anomie by going back to our lost Paradise because it no longer exists.[1]

2. Does it make any difference if scientists try to explain the data of science by referring also to mystical, spiritual or transcendental connections? In the following statement Fritjof Capra compares Buddha and the bomb. How could we make a linkage between Jesus and our modern technological ability?

   > The connection between physics and mysticism is not only very interesting but also extremely important. Because we have to put it into the present cultural perspective, into the perspective of the values of the current culture. Now what are the values of our culture? Well, look at what scientists are doing. Half of our scientists and engineers today work for the military. In my lectures I often say that modern physics can lead us to

the Buddha or to the bomb. It's up to us to choose one of these paths. And it seems to me that at a time when so much scientific work is wasted by using an enormous potential of human ingenuity and creativity to develop even more sophisticated means of total destruction, that the paradigm of the Buddha cannot be overemphasized. This seems to me to be very crucial. Therefore, to link science to mysticism does not take away anything from its grandeur. On the contrary, it ennobles science, and in our present situation, because of the nuclear threat, it may well be crucial to the survival of humanity.[2]

3. Read Genesis 1:1–9. Then reflect on the comment of Allen Utke:

> . . . we seem to once again be at a point in history where we may have become "too big for our britches." We are once again priding ourselves as being the most intelligent, knowledgeable, practical, cosmopolitan, "advanced" men in history. And once again we are at work building massive monuments to our glory.[3]

*   *   *

See Scrapbook, pages 6,16, 30, 31, 32, 34, 35 and 43 for additional discussion material.

RELATIONSHIPS

ASSUMPTIONS

Would you change or add to any of the following?

1. *Degradation*

   In our experience of the world, mystery has been degraded by our overdependence on technology. The acceptance of and participation in mystery is essential to healthy living.

2. *Wholeness*

   There are deeper secrets and callings in life than just those of rational science and pragmatic technology. We are not called to reject science or technology but rather to recognize that any one aspect of human endeavor or experience is but a part. The journey should be toward wholeness; it should not be a single-minded pursuit, whether of technology alone *or* mysticism alone.

3. *Participation*

   The "great slow gestures of trees" are as essential to us as the physical characteristics of silicon chips as we seek information about our existence. We need to seriously ponder the difference between the trees, which are a part of the evolutionary ethic, and the silicon chips, which are a human creation. There is more to both than mere explanation.

4. *Meaning*

Physicists have discovered that when they attempt to describe the realm of atoms they have to resort to descriptions and categories very similar to those used by mystics. This is not, however, a failure of science. It is the recognition that scientific explanations are not the only explanations with "true" meaning. The challenge is how to let mystery back into our sense of meaning.

QUESTIONS

1. Is there any place for mystery in a technological world? If so or if not, give reasons and examples.

2. If we take seriously the Gaia hypothesis and the idea of "the Earth as a living being" — and change our outlook on nature from that of the survival of the fittest to that of biological cooperation — what might that do to our technology?

3. As we seek an image to guide our relationships with people of other cultures, would it make any sense to see it as Henri Nouwen suggests: "It is the change from selling pearls to hunting for the treasure."

4. Do you believe it is possible to adopt the technological philosophy and practice of "thinking globally and acting locally?" Examples?

5. What is your view of "wholeness" in relationship to God's creation?

QUOTATIONS

1. Should we begin to consider seriously that there are some things we *can* do that we should *not* do? What ideas come to mind from Fritjof Capra's thoughts on *wu wei?*

    The term *wu wei* is frequently used in Taoist philosophy and means literally 'nonaction'. In the West the term is usually interpreted as referring to passivity. This is quite wrong. What the Chinese mean by *wu wei* is not abstaining from activity but abstaining from a certain kind of activity, activity that is out of harmony with the ongoing cosmic process.[2]

2. Do you think Arthur Waskow is right in his comparison of "Mastery" and "Mystery"? What do you think of his suggestion for taking seriously our relationship to each other and to creation?

> When secularism asserts that the human race is now Master of the Universe, and that in principle there is no more Mystery—only temporary ignorance—it is asserting a partial truth as if it were an Absolute Truth. That assertion is what many religious traditions called idolatry—and as the Psalms say, those who make idols will become like them: dead. The deadly idolatry of asserting human Mastery and denying Mystery is well on the way to destroying the human race— well on the way to a universal death.
>
> Imagine that in every laboratory or social-science seminar or class in business administration, as work is about to begin, a one-month old baby is passed around the room from hand to hand, and each scientist, scholar, student, administrator says aloud: 'What we are about to do, to think, to plan, to learn, we do simply in order that you should grow up to be as old as we are.'[3]

3. Read 2 Corinthians 5:16–21. Reflect on how the "old" passing away into the "new" means that we are called to shift our point of view if we are to be reconcilers and ambassadors for Christ. Does that have any connection to relationships in a technological world?

*   *   *

See Scrapbook, pages 7, 10, 11, 21, 24, 25, 26, 62, 63, 70 and 71 for additional discussion material.

SESSION FOUR

THE SUBJECTIVE COMPUTER

ASSUMPTIONS

Would you change or add to any of the following?

1. *Mind*

   The use of computers is redefining how and what we think about ourselves. The program in a computer becomes, in effect, another mind to interact with, and so our concept of mind is changing.

2. *Personality*

   The computer is not the same thing to all people. It has the ability to become an extension of one's personality, which means that it has the ability to change one's personality.

3. *Authority*

   The computer has made possible the existence of a "third person" authority, i.e., the computer did it or made me do it. What ordinary users of computers do not have access to is the "rules of the game" that are fed into computers—for example, the rules governing military responses to real or perceived threats.

4. *Information*

   The generation and manipulation of data about ourselves and the world, whether it has to do with our salaries or the migratory patterns of animals, puts other important information out of the picture—information that is not "data" in the sense of stored numbers: such as information on job satisfaction, or our mystical, spiritual relationships with the animals in our environment.

QUESTIONS

1. Describe your experience with computers. Has it had any impact on how you think about yourself and the world you live in? If so, describe the impact.

2. In what ways are computers changing the circumstances and expectations of our daily lives? Which ones do you like and which ones do you not like?

3. Do you approve of surveillance systems that allow computers to use a social security number to track down a deserting father or mother? What about to track down a person who failed to make car payments? Can you provide other examples that you would approve or disapprove of?

4. Do you think computers will radically change the way we think about ourselves in the future? Illustrate your answer.

5. Do you think computers will ever be accepted as "intelligent" in the same way we accept humans as "intelligent?" If yes or no, do you think this would be a good development?

QUOTATIONS:

1. What impact do you foresee, knowing that children are growing up with computers as *the* way and not as a *different* way? Do you identify with Sarah in the following quotation? Sarah, a thirty-five year old lawyer and mother of three, is talking about the gap between herself and her son:

   I could have learned that 'new math.' I could understand, respect my son if his values turn out to be different than mine. I mean, I think I could handle the kinds of things that came up between parents and kids in the sixties. I would have talked to my son: I would have tried to understand. But my ten-year-old is into programming, into computers, and I feel that this makes his mind work in a whole different way.[1]

2. What is your reaction to the following two illustrations of computer "evolution"?

Jerry Mander:
> A skillful video-game player stimulates the computer program to go faster, and as the circle speeds up (computer program to nervous system to hands to machine to computer program) the player becomes as one with the machine. They become connected in one fluid cycle, aspects of each other. Over time, and with practice, the abilities of the human being develop to approximate the computer program. Evolution is furthered by this sort of interaction, but it is of a notably different form than prior evolutionary processes. Where evolution was once an interaction between humans and nature, it now takes place between human and human artifacts. We co-evolve with the environment which we have created—with our machines. We co-evolve, that is, with ourselves. It's a kind of inbreeding, and it makes us think nature is increasingly irrelevant to us.[2]

Jeremy Rifkin:
> Within the coming decade, the computer industry and the life sciences are expected to join together in a new field, molecular electronics. Companies like Japan's Mitsui Corporation are already planning for that day by acquiring ' a large stake in both biotechnology and microelectronics. ' The grand objective is to turn living material into biocomputers and then to use these biocomputers to further engineer living materials. In the future, biocomputers will be engineered directly into living systems, just as micro-computers are engineered into mechanical systems today. They will monitor activity, adjust performance, speed up and slow down metabolic activity, transform living material into products, and perform a host of other supervisory functions. Scientists even envision the day when computers made out of living material will automatically reproduce themselves, finally blurring the last remaining distinction between living and mechanical processes.[3]

3. Select and read two or three psalms that are pleasing to you. Then reflect on how computers have brought into existence new languages—new expressions of mind, if you will. The point is not to think about computers someday writing psalms, but rather

how language communicates. Will computer languages ever communicate something about God? Or vice versa: does God communicate something about computer languages?

*   *   *

See Scrapbook, pages 28, 36, 37, 38, 39, 42, 47, 64 and 65 for additional discussion material.

SESSION FIVE

REMODELING OUR GENES

ASSUMPTIONS

Would you change or add to any of the following?

1. *Human Creation*

   The technological imperative is moving from the improvement of human health to the remodeling or redesigning of human beings. Because there is no place in the current notion of technological progress for matters like spirit, compassion, love or justice, to allow genetic engineering to be directed only by scientists and technologists is to ensure disaster.

2. *Restraint*

   The fundamental question in genetic engineering is not a technological question but a values question: Are there some things we know how to do that we should *not* do?

3. *Choice*

   Because of advances in technology, the stage has already shifted from one of having babies to one of having *healthy* babies. The possibility of "optimal" babies means that some values will be chosen over others — and the choices will be made by scientists, not the public — much less the poor.

4. *The Poor*

    The use of technologies of energy and agriculture have not yet shown they will make a significant difference for the masses of the poor, and so we must ask: what will be the burden of genetic technologies on the poor?

QUESTIONS

1. Do you favor or oppose the attempt to create a "second" nature — a new species created by human choice? Give reasons.

2. What are the pros and cons of genetic engineering as it relates to profit-making economics?

3. Should we begin to discuss seriously the possibilities of linking science and love, or is that just a romantic idea?

4. Should we develop the technology of cloning, that is, the reproduction from a single cell, so that if parents lost a child in an accident they could "grow" another that would be genetically identical?

5. Should we mix human and animal genes in living organisms? For example, what if we learned how to implant genes from a mouse into a growing human fetus so that the resulting child would be totally resistant to cancer?

QUOTATIONS

1. Which of the following two viewpoints are you most comfortable with, that of Arno Motulsky or that of Leon Kass? Are they mutually exclusive or can they be combined? If exclusive, why? If combined, how?

    Motulsky:
    > The new biological revolution based on DNA has been with us for only one generation and genetic manipulation by gene splicing was developed less than 10 years ago. Neither scientists nor the public in general have absorbed the full impact of these developments. As more is learned about DNA and

human genetics more problems are certain to arise. Nevertheless, well-informed human beings in enlightened democratic societies should foster the use of the new DNA technology in a responsible manner that will lead to better health and welfare for all.[1]

Kass:

We have paid some high prices for the technological conquest of nature, but none perhaps so high as the intellectual and spiritual costs of seeing nature as mere material for our manipulation, exploitation and transformation. With the power for biological engineering now gathering, there will be splendid new opportunities for a similar degradation of our view of man. Indeed, we are already witnessing the erosion of our idea of man as something splendid or divine, as a creature with freedom and dignity. And clearly, if we come to see ourselves as meat, then meat we shall become.[2]

2. What kinds of safeguards or checkpoints should we develop so that, as Chet Fuller writes, we do not overrun our headlights? In response to the announcement of U.S. Department of Agriculture experiments with human genes and pigs and sheep, Fuller asks:

Why do we need sheep as big as cows, or pigs as big as horses, anyway? . . . if mice keep getting bigger, won't we also have to increase the size of cats? . . . It is not that we need to end our pursuit of the mysteries of life, but that we need to establish some kind of realistic speed limits so that while traveling the dark and tricky tunnels of the unknown we don't keep overrunning our headlights.[3]

3. As one might expect, two biblical passages that clearly relate to questions of genetic engineering are the creation stories in Genesis (1:1–2–4 and 2:5–25). What would it mean to be faithful to these biblical stories? If we were to begin a "second" creation, what would we be faithful to? Would there be any purpose to such a creation other than just the technological grandeur? Read Daniel 3:1–18 about Shadrach, Meschach, and Abednego. Reflect on the fact that the issue for them was not survival, but remaining faithful to God. Then reflect on the issue of genetic engineering not as creation, but as being faithful to God. In other words, what faithfulness should undergird any attempts at refashioning God's creation? Finally, turn to Genesis, Chapter 3,

for further reflection on the consequences of God's creation of human beings. What is faithfulness in the creation issue for us?

*   *   *

See Scrapbook, pages 16, 17, 28, 48, 49, 50, 51, 52, 53, 58, 59 and 69 for additional discussion material.

SESSION SIX

THE NUCLEAR GENIE

ASSUMPTIONS

Would you change or add to any of the following?

1. *Power*

   The human desire for power has become a theological dilemma growing out of nuclear technology. Although the quest to play God is as old as humankind, we have now acquired the power to destroy life on earth through nuclear weapons.

2. *Spirit*

   Nuclear technology, whether it is used for weapons or to produce energy, gives rise to spiritual as well as intellectual questions. And the spiritual answer is clearly that we should do without it.

3. *Sin*

   The use of nuclear technologies causes us to sin because we know what is right but fail to do it. We know it is not right to put incredible lasting burdens on nature through radioactive wastes; we know it is not right to hold the peoples of the earth hostage to superpowers aiming enough nuclear weaponry at each other to kill every human twenty times over.

4. *Alternatives*

   There are viable, sane options to nuclear weapons and nuclear energy: nuclear disarmament and solar energy.

QUESTIONS

1. Do you accept or reject the idea that on Christian grounds, the use of nuclear technology for weapons and energy is unacceptable? Explain your view.

2. Do you accept or reject the view that we do not need nuclear energy because solar energy provides a viable alternative, and what is lacking is only the political will to make the shift? We had the Manhattan Project to develop nuclear technology and the Apollo Project to develop space technology, so why not a Prometheus Project to change our energy source to solar? Amplify your view.

3. Do you agree or disagree that the invention of the nuclear bomb has killed war and that the task before humankind is to learn how to resolve differences without resort to killing each other? Amplify your view.

4. What is your view of the Soviet Union? Does it make any difference to you that there are forty million Russian Orthodox Christians and around one million Baptist and Pentecostal Christians in the Soviet Union?

5. What is your view of the fact that although it has become more difficult to build nuclear power plants in the U.S. because of cost and environmental concerns, U.S. companies continue to export nuclear technology to other countries?

QUOTATIONS

1. What steps can you take to "untie the chain" that Steve Baer writes about?

    A dog that hasn't been chained up long forgets. It rushes across the yard and then—bang. Today when people become excited about the future and involve themselves with new uses of technology they often get carried away with hope—then bam—they think about the bomb, the H bomb, the ballistic missile. Today, like the dog, we all have the chain on us. There is nothing very marvelous going on unless it is something to untie that chain.[1]

2. What do you think of the following argument that Jacques Ellul makes?

> Jesus reproached the Pharisees because they made God's law into an iron yoke for people, a total constraint; they made the commandment into an objective duty; they made detailed prescriptions so that there was no longer any room for initiative. They made the free Word of God into an inflexible, systematic code. Jesus came to bring flexibility, adaptability, and freedom back into it. In this way, the law of God (which, as James says, is ' the law of freedom ') is truly honored.
>
> The law of God has become a social system. By analogy, any system that leads to inflexibility goes against the will of God. Dictatorship, wherever it is found and in whatever form, is unacceptable to the Christian, because it is a rigid system leaving no free room among its structures, no place for initiative. Nuclear development and its institutional, economic, and social rigidity should also be recognized as unacceptable.[2]

3. Read Amos, Chapter 5 on God's call to repentance. Reflect on the possibility that we might repent of our development of nuclear technologies that carry significant possibility of the destruction of the environment and human life. Then make a connection between our own "religious festivals" (to use Amos' term) and our doing what is "right".

*   *   *

See Scrapbook, pages 19, 36, 37, 38 and 39 for additional discussion material.

SESSION SEVEN

THE TWO-THIRDS WORLD

ASSUMPTIONS

Would you change or add to any of the following?

1. *Sufficiency*

   What we need is a technology of sufficiency, a technology that recognizes both ecological and human balance. Technological development must consider many frameworks of balance; that is, it must consider compassion as well as efficiency, dignity as well as profit.

2. *Change*

   A basic assumption of progress that needs change is that the poor countries need to become as industrialized as developed countries. This does not mean freezing out the poor from the benefits of technology; it means a change in technologies for the rich and the poor. The important question is: What would happen if, instead of trying to change the poor, we changed the technologies all of us use?

3. *Experience*

   We cannot determine how to change technology until we re-experience the poor. If we who are not materially poor were to enter into the situation of the poor, experience their wisdom and try to understand their worldview, changes in our social, political and economic systems would be inevitable; so would be changes in the technologies we use and create.

QUESTIONS

1. What is your attitude toward the Two-Thirds World? What do you think of the view that as a person from the industrialized world you have more to receive from the Two-Thirds World than you have to give? In light of this, is there any significant change required of you? Amplify your answer.

2. Many people agree that the solution to world hunger is political, not technological. We already have the technological capability to feed the world; it is our political/social/economic systems that keep it from happening. Do you agree or disagree with this position?

3. How can we expect to know what to do about the poor if we have no direct experience of their situation? Unless we experience what it is like to be poor, won't we just try to make "them" like "us"?

4. Do you think poor people will ever get a robot? How can we seek ways to change the relationship between economics and technology so that the goal will not be economic growth and profit, but helping all people. Technologies based on preventive health care, for example, do not require economic growth and profit. Can you think of other examples?

5. Should we try to develop technologies that make *shalom* rather than money? Or should we continue to export our present technologies to Two-Thirds World countries? Amplify your view.

QUOTATIONS

1. How does our technological way of life speak to others? Are we trapped or can we take some initial steps out of it? What do you think of the following quotation by James Robertson:

    > For instance, if you fly by jet plane all over the world to tell people that they should use bicycles instead of energy-expensive transport, is your message likely to be more effective than your example, or vice versa? If you take up self-sufficient organic farming, after making a lot of money as a stockbroker, which of the two ways of life will you be an advertisement for?[1]

2. To marginalize something, whether it is the environment or the poor, is to say by our actions that it does not count. But these things do not go away; sooner or later they have to be dealt with. Describe some examples of "sacred wholeness" as it is explained in the following quotation:

> I remember a black man trying to impress this sense of sacred wholeness upon a bishop. Bishop, he said, the world is *round*. You can't sweep people off the edge when you're through with them. You can't sweep your garbage off the edge either. The world is round, and sooner or later, if you try to sweep things over the edge, they gonna come back up around the other side and bat your ass![2]

3. Read Mary's song of praise in Luke 1:46–55. Reflect on a message of gladness and promise that turns the normal order of things upside down. Think of this song not as a realignment of eternal spiritual values but as a political and social reversal. Is God calling us to action that liberates the poor? Action which offers us true freedom—the turning around to be servants?

*　*　*

See Scrapbook, pages 14, 15, 30, 31, 32, 33, 66 and 67 for additional discussion material.

PIONEERING AND FAITHFULNESS

ASSUMPTIONS

Would you change or add to any of the following?

1. *Living/Thinking*

   We must learn to live our way into a new way of thinking, not think our way into a new way of living. By becoming pioneers in the way we live we can inform the way we think.

2. *Prayer and Silence*

   We must spend more time in prayer and silence pondering the recognition that the old won't do—that we are called to love, not to seek a success based on material security.

3. *Passion for Quality*

   We must acquire a passion for quality and wholeness; we must understand how what we do affects those who are "left out."

4. *Faithfulness*

   To invent the future we must struggle with what we need, not simply *do* all that we can do. Our two greatest needs are first, learning how and when to say no, technologically. And second, placing faithfulness to God's calling through Jesus Christ above technological grandeur.

QUESTIONS

1. Why does there seem to be an absence, today, of heroines or heroes to inspire people to rise toward greatness? Persons like Clara Barton, who started the Red Cross; Dorothy Day, who carried the cause of the worker and of peace; Gandhi and Martin Luther King, Jr. who demonstrated the power of nonviolent resistance? Why is there an absence, today, of powerful, motivating ideas like "go West" or the U.S. Bill of Rights? Do you think there are any great people and ideas alive today? Give examples if you do. If you think not, what does that do to your sense of the future?

2. What do you think "quality" is? Work at defining and giving examples of quality. Is your definition attainable? If so, will you attain it? If not, why have a definition of quality that is unattainable?

3. What, to you, does "faithfulness" mean? Work at defining faithfulness; give examples. Is your definition attainable? If so, will you attain it? If not, why have a definition of faithfulness that is unattainable?

4. Would you be willing to reformulate your life around an attitude of Christian pioneering? For example, should we pioneer the attitude—and practice—that the test of technology is what happens to the poor? If so, how would you start?

5. Do you agree or disagree with the idea that we are called to invent new ways "out of the quiet recognition that the old won't do?" Illustrate.

QUOTATIONS

1. Do you agree with the following idea of E. F. Schumacher? If you do not, what will you do instead? If you do agree, what steps are you going to take?

   Everywhere people ask: 'What can I actually *do*?' The answer is as simple as it is disconcerting: we can, each of us, work to put our own inner house in order. The guidance we need for this work cannot be found in science or technology, the value of which utterly depends on the ends they serve; but it can still be found in the traditional wisdom of mankind.[1]

2. Is it crazy to believe and act upon the idea that it is possible to "invent peace" and "end the arms trade?" And that the time to do both is now? Why or why not? How do you react to the following thoughts of Norman Cousins and Roger Walsh?

    Norman Cousins:

    > I don't think that we're called upon in the world today to do the impossible. I don't think we're called upon to move the mountains or raise the plains or rearrange the planets in the skies. I think that we're called upon to be responsible. I think we're called upon to be imaginative. I think we're called upon to be sensitive to the needs of life and to give a proper value to life. And finally, I think we're called upon to prove that since war is an invention of the human mind that the human mind can invent peace.[2]

    Roger Walsh:

    > ' The idea that [the arms trade] can be eliminated is ridiculous '; ' So many people, industries, and nations are dependent on it that there would be widespread economic collapse '; ' People would never agree to abolishing it. ' Do these arguments sound familiar? They should! They were staunchly believed and vehemently fought for only a century ago in response to talk of abolishing slavery. Today slavery is not only abolished, but almost universally abhorred. Yet today the arms trade kills more people every few years than the slave trade did over centuries. One reason for this is that we believe the arms trade is acceptable, even essential, exactly as our forefathers believed about the slave trade.[3]

3. The New Testament is a rich source for pioneering ideas, for bringing into existence that which is not yet. Examples: Luke 10:25–37, on giving mercy and compassion to our enemies; Luke 9:28–43, on experiencing the holy in the Transfiguration and returning to the needy through casting out a demon; Matthew 25:31–46, on the judgement of those who do not feed the hungry and give drink to the thirsty. Read also Acts 5:29, 1 Corinthians 2:5, and 1 Corinthians 1:27. Reflect on pioneering and faithfulness with regard to obeying God, having faith in God's power and recognizing what is foolish.

*   *   *

See Scrapbook, pages 4, 5, 8, 9, 14, 15, 26, 28, 40, 43, 44, 46, 68 and 75 for additional discussion material.

FOOTNOTES

Introduction

[1] Quoted in Ken Wilber, ed., *The Holographic Paradigm and Other Paradoxes,* (Boulder, Colorado: Shambhala, 1982), pp. 15–16.

[2] Khellog Albran, *The Profit,* (Los Angeles: Price/Stern/Sloan, 1981), p. 35.

[3] Kosuke Koyama, *Three Mile an Hour God,* (Maryknoll, New York: Orbis Books, 1979), p.7.

Prologue

[1] Carlos Fuentes, "High Noon in Latin America," *Vanity Fair*, September, 1983.

[2] Rachel Carson, *Silent Spring*, (New York: Houghton Mifflin Company, 1962).

[3] Kurt Baier and Nicholas Rescher, eds., *Values and the Future,* (New York: The Free Press, 1969), p. 5.

[4] Richard Schaull, *Heralds of a New Reformation: The Poor of South and North America,* (Maryknoll, New York: Orbis Books, 1984), p. 110.

[5] Barbara Tuchmann, *The March of Folly,* (New York: Alfred A. Knopf, 1984), p. 8.

[6] Paul Davies, *God and the New Physics,* (New York: Simon and Schuster, 1983), p. 2.

[7] Ken Cauthen, *The Ethics of Enjoyment,* (Atlanta: John Knox Press, 1975), p. 1.

[8] Stephen Geyer, "Dreams," © 1982 Backwood Music, Inc./Dar-JEN Music on John Denver Album, "Seasons of the Heart," © 1982 RCA Records.

[9] Ivan Illich, *Shadow Work,* (Boston: Marion Boyars, 1981), p. 9.

[10] Robert Pirsig, *Zen and the Art of Motorcycle Maintenance,* (New York: Bantam Books, 1974), p. 284.

[11] *Ibid,* p. 158.

[12] J. R. R. Tolkien, *The Fellowship of the Ring,* (New York: Ballantine Books, 1965), p. 353.

[13] Norman Cousins, "Lunar Meditations," *Saturday Review*, August 14, 1971, p. 20.

One

[1] Jacques Ellul, *The Technological System,* (New York, Continuum, 1980), p. 48.

[2] Theodore Roszak, *Where the Wasteland Ends: Politics and Transcendence in Postindustrial Society,* (New York: Doubleday, 1972), p. 373.

[3] See Lynn Margulis and James E. Lovelock, "The Atmosphere as Circulatory System of the Biosphere—The Gaia Hypothesis," *The Coevolution Quarterly,* Summer, 1975, pp. 31–40. And Norman Myers, ed., *Gaia, An Atlas of Planet Management,* (Garden City, New York: Anchor Press, 1984).

[4] Nancy Jack Todd and John Todd, *Bioshelters, Ocean Arks, City Farming: Ecology as the Basis of Design,* (San Francisco: Sierra Club Books, 1984), p. 13.

[5] Samuel C. Florman, *The Existential Pleasures of Engineering,* (New York: St. Martin's Press, 1976), p. 147.

[6] *Ibid,* p. 122.

[7] *Ibid,* p. 130.

[8] *Ibid,* p. 138.

[9] Todd and Todd, p. 17.

[10] Quoted in Robert McAfee Brown, *Unexpected News: Reading the Bible with Third World Eyes,* (Philadelphia: Westminster Press, 1984), p. 141.

[11] Theodore Roszak, "The Manifesto of the Person," *New Directions,* Spring, 1978, p. 22.

Two

[1] Quoted in *World Press Review,* November, 1984, p. 54.

[2] Kirkpatrick Sale, *Human Scale,* (New York: Coward, McCann and Geoghegan, 1980), p. 60.

[3] Henri J. M. Nouwen, *¡Gracias!: A Latin American Journal,* (New York: Harper & Row, 1983), p. 62.

[4] Leopold Kohr, *The Breakdown of Nations,* (New York: Dutton, 1978, American Edition), pp. xviii.

[5] R. D. Laing, *Conversations with Adam and Natasha,* (New York: Pantheon Books, 1977), p. 81.

[6] Sale, p. 27f.

[7] E. F. Schumacher, *Small is Beautiful,* (New York: Harper & Row, 1973), p. 21.

[8] *Ibid,* p. 185.

[9] Quoted in Ken Darrow and Rick Pam, *Appropriate Technology Sourcebook,* (Stanford, California: Volunteers in Asia, 1976), p. 9.

[10] Quoted in James M. Wall, "Combating Science On Death and Dying." *The Christian Century,* August 1–8, 1984, p. 731.

[11] *Ibid.*

[12] Wendell Berry, *The Unsettling of America: Culture & Agriculture,* (New York: Avon Books, 1977), p. 222.

[13] *Ibid,* p. 223.

[14] Norman Myers, ed., *Gaia, An Atlas of Planet Management,* (Garden City, New York: Anchor Press, 1984).

[15] See Schumacher, "Technology With a Human Face," p. 138f.

[16] Robin Clarke in *The Futurist,* Dec., 1974, p. 268.

[17] John V. Taylor, *Enough is Enough,* (Minneapolis: Augsburg Publishing House, 1977), p. 93.

[18] Berry, p. 7f.

[19] Schumacher, p. 31.

Three

[1] Samuel C. Florman, *The Existential Pleasures of Engineering,* (New York: St. Martin's Press, 1976), p. 65.

[2] Ursula K. LeGuin, *A Wizard of Earthsea,* (New York: Ace Books, 1968), p. 98.

[3] Jacques Ellul, *The Technological System*, (New York: Continuum, 1980), p. 48.

[4] Fritjof Capra, *The Tao of Physics,* (New York: Bantam Books, 1975), p. 4.

[5] *Ibid,* p. 27.

[6] *Ibid,* p. 23.

[7] *Ibid,* p. 70.

[8] *Ibid,* p. 294.

[9] Robert McAfee Brown, *Unexpected News: Reading the Bible with Third World Eyes,* (Philadelphia: Westminster Press, 1984), p. 27.

[10] John V. Taylor, *Enough is Enough,* (Minneapolis: Augsburg Publishing House, 1977), p. 41.

[11] Lewis Thomas, *Late Night Thoughts on Listening to Mahler's Ninth Symphony,* (New York: Bantam Books, 1983), p. 105.

[12] *Ibid.*

[13] Loren Eiseley, *The Immense Journey,* (New York: Vintage Books, 1956, 1957), p. 195.

[14] *Ibid,* p. 208.

[15] *Ibid.*

Four

[1] Douglas R. Hofstadtner, *Godel, Escher, Bach: An Eternal Golden Braid,* (New York: Vintage Books, 1979), p. 406.

[2] Gregory Bateson, *Steps to an Ecology of Mind,* (New York: Ballantine Books, 1972), p. 476.

[3] Quoted in Alvin Toffler, *The Third Wave,* (New York: William Morrow and Co., 1980), p. 130.

[4] Jerry Mander, "Six Grave Doubts about Computers," *Whole Earth Review,* January, 1985, p. 11f.

[5] Sherry Turkle, *The Second Self: Computers and the Human Spirit,* (New York: Simon and Schuster, 1984), p. 13.

[6] Craig Brod, *Technostress: The Human Cost of the Computer Revolution,* (New York, Addison-Wesley, 1984), p. 47.

[7] Turkle, p. 92.

[8] Stewart Brand, Ed., *Whole Earth Software Catalog,* (New York: Quantum Press/ Double-day, 1984), p. 4.

[9] Turkle, p. 105f.

[10] *Ibid,* p. 146

[11] *Ibid,* 152.

[12] Mander, p. 13.

[13] *Ibid.*

[14] *Ibid,* p. 16.

[15] *Ibid,* p. 17.

[16] David Burnham, *The Rise of the Computer State,* (New York: Vintage Books, 1984), p. 88.

[17] *Ibid.*

[18] Langdon Winner, "Mythinformation," *Whole Earth Review,* January, 1985, p. 22.

[19] Mander, p. 20.

[20] As quoted in Burnham, p. 186.

[21] Brand, p. 2.

[22] Turkle, p. 173.

[23] *Ibid.*

Five

1 Jeremy Rifkin, *Algeny: A New Word—A New World*, (New York: Penquin Books, 1984), Author's note.

2 Quoted in *Chemical and Engineering News,* April 7, 1980, p. 6.

3 *The Wit and Wisdom of Archie Bunker,* (New York: Popular Library, 1971), p. 15.

4 Daniel Callahan, "The Moral Career of Genetic Engineering," *The Hastings Center Report*, April, 1979, p. 9.

5 *Ibid,* p. 21.

6 *Ibid.*

7 Quoted in Nicholas Wade, *The Ultimate Experiment: Man-Made Evolution*, (New York: Walker and Company, 1977), p. 113.

8 Theodore Roszak, "The Monster and the Titan: Science, Knowledge, and Gnosis," *Daedalus*, Summer, 1974, p. 30.

9 *Ibid,* p. 31.

10 Rifkin, p. 244.

11 *Ibid.*

Six

1 Morris Berman, *The Reenchantment of the World,* (New York: Bantam Books, 1984), p. 173.

2 Wendell Berry, *A Continuous Harmony,* (New York: Harcourt Brace Jovanovich, 1970, 1972), p. 97.

3 Wendell Berry, *The Unsettling of America: Culture & Agriculture,* (New York: Avon Books, 1977), p. 97.

4 Loren Eiseley, *The Immense Journey*, (New York: Vintage Books, 1956, 1957), p. 180.

5 Ursula K. LeGuin, *A Wizard Of Earthsea*, (New York: Ace Books, 1968), p. 56f.

6 *Ibid.*

7 Jonathan Schell, *The Abolition*, (New York: Alfred A. Knopf, 1984), p. 3.

8 *Ibid.*

9 Jonathan Schell, *The Fate of the Earth,* (New York: Alfred A. Knopf, 1982), p. 17f.

10 Schell, *The Abolition*, p. 17.

11 Schell, *The Fate Of The Earth*, p. 8.

12 *Ibid.*

[13] Quoted in Harold Willens, *The Trimtab Factor*, (New York: William Morrow & Co., 1984), p. 72.

[14] Schell, *The Abolition*, p. 5f.

[15] Jacques Ellul, "Unabridged Spirit of Power," *Sojourners*, July–August, 1982, p. 14f.

Seven

[1] George Chaplin and Glenn D. Piage, eds., *Hawaii 2000*, (Honolulu: University Press of Hawaii, 1973), p. 133f.

[2] John V. Taylor, *Enough is Enough*, (Minneapolis: Augsburg Publishing House, 1977), p. 6.

[3] *Ibid*, p. 28.

[4] Idries Shah, *The Subtleties of the Inimitable Mulla Nasrudin*, (New York: E. P. Dutton & Co., Inc., 1973), p 101

[5] Article in *Atlanta Constitution*, Jan. 3, 1985, p. 1A.

[6] Exodus 16:3.

[7] Exodus 16:18.

[8] William Stringfellow, "An Assault Upon Conscience," *Sojourners*, Oct., 1984, p. 25.

[9] Jim Wallis, *Agenda for Biblical People*, (New York: Harper & Row, 1984), p. 66.

[10] Henri J. M. Nouwen, *¡Gracias!: A Latin American Journal*, (New York: Harper & Row, 1983), p. 22.

[11] George McRobie, *Small is Possible*, (New York: Harper & Row, 1981), p. 1.

[12] McRobie, p. 3.

[13] Kirkpatrick Sale, *Human Scale*, (New York: Coward, McCann & Geoghegan, 1980), p. 161.

[14] E. F. Schumacher, *Small is Beautiful: Economics as if People Mattered*, (New York: Harper & Row, 1973), p. 145.

Eight

[1] Wendell Berry, *The Memory of Old Jack*, (New York: Harcourt Brace Jovanovich, 1974), p. 143.

[2] *Ibid.*

[3] James Robertson, *The Sane Alternative: A Choice Of Futures*, (St. Paul, Minnesota: River Basin Publishing Co., 1979), p. 18.

[4] *Ibid*, p. 88.

[5] *Ibid.*

[6] Frank Herbert, *Children of Dune,* (New York: Berkley Publishing Corporation, 1976), p. 116.

[7] Robert Pirsig, *Zen and the Art of Motorcycle Maintenance,* (New York: Bantam Books, 1974), p. 352.

[8] *Ibid,* p. 18.

[9] Loren Eiseley, *The Invisible Pyramid,* (New York: Charles Scribner's Sons, 1970), p. 82f.

[10] E. F. Schumacher, *Small is Beautiful,* (New York: Harper & Row, 1973), p. 61f.

[11] Paul Hawken, James Ogilvy, Peter Schwartz, *Seven Tomorrows,* (New York: Bantam Books, 1982), p. 8.

[12] John Naisbitt, *Megatrends,* (New York: Warner Books, 1982), p. 87.

[13] Theodore Roszak, *Unfinished Animal,* (New York: Harper & Row, 1975), p. 47.

[14] Ivan Illich, *Deschooling Society,* (New York: Penguin Books, 1971), p. 111f.

[15] Job 38: 16,25a,33,34; 39:19a

[16] Richard Schaull, *Heralds of a New Reformation: The Poor of South and North America,* (Maryknoll, New York: Orbis Books, 1984), p. 88.

[17] *Ibid,* p. 13f.

[18] *Ibid,* p. 35.

[19] *Ibid,* p. 28.

[20] Jacques Ellul, *The Technological System,* (New York: Continuum, 1980), p. 324.

[21] Ariel Dorfman, *The Empire's Old Clothes,* (New York: Pantheon Books, 1983), p. 3.

[22] *Ibid,* p. 4.

[23] *Ibid.*

[24] *Ibid,* p. 5.

[25] Marvin Cetron and Thomas O'Toole, *Encounters with the Future: A Forecast of Life into the 21st Century,* (New York: McGraw-Hill Book Company, 1982), p. 296.

[26] *Ibid,* p. 295.

[27] *Ibid,* p. 299.

[28] *Ibid,* p. 17.

[29] *Ibid.*

[30] *Ibid.*

[31] *Ibid,* p. 3.

[32] Kurt Vonnegut, Jr. *Mother Night*, (New York: Bard Books, 1961, 1966), p. v.

[33] Marilyn Ferguson, *The Aquarian Conspiracy: Personal and Social Transformation in the 1980's,* (Los Angeles: J. P. Tarcher, Inc., 1980), p. 37.

Postscript

[1] Russell Hoban, *Riddley Walker*, (New York: Summit Books, 1980), p. 186.

[2] *Ibid,* p. 154.

[3] Quoted in *The Aquarian Conspiracy: Personal and Social Transformation in the 1980's,* (Los Angeles: J. P. Tarcher, Inc., 1980), p. 50.

[4] Frank Herbert, *Dune Messiah,* (New York: Berkley Publishing Corporation, 1969), p. 162.

[5] Hoban, p. 207.

LEADER'S GUIDE

One

[1] Herman Kahn, William Brown, and Leon Martel, *The Next Two Hundred Years*, (New York: William Morrow and Co., 1976), p. 1, 7.

[2] George T. Lock Land, *Grow or Die*, (New York: Random House, 1973), p. 74.

[3] Samuel Florman, *The Existential Pleasures of Engineering*, (New York: St. Martin's Press, 1976), p. 77f.

Two

[1] R. Gibellini, ed., *Frontiers of Theology in Latin America,* (Maryknoll, New York: Orbis Books, 1979), p. 291.

[2] Quoted in Ken Wilbert, ed., *The Holographic Paradigm and Other Paradoxes,* (Boulder, Colorado: Shambhala, 1982), p. 229.

[3] Allen P. Utke, *Bio-Babel: Can We Survive the New Biology?*, (Atlanta: John Knox Press, 1978), p. 116.

Three

[1] Henri J. M. Nouwen, *¡Gracias!: A Latin American Journal*, (New York: Harper & Row, 1983), p. 7.

[2] Fritjof Capra, *The Turning Point: Science, Society, and the Rising Culture*, (New York, Bantam Books, 1982), p. 37.

[3] Arthur Waskow, "Mystery Not Mastery", *The CoEvolution Quarterly*, Fall, 1983, p. 45.

Four

[1] Sherry Turkle, *The Second Self: Computers and the Human Spirit*, (New York: Simon and Schuster, 1984), p. 95.

[2] Jerry Mander, "Six Grave Doubts about Computers", *Whole Earth Review,* Jan., 1985, p. 18.

[3] Jeremy Rifkin, *Algeny: A New Word — A New World*, (New York, Penguin Books, 1984), p. 22.

Five

[1] Arno G. Motulsky, "Impact of Genetic Manipulation on Society and Medicine", *Science*, January 14, 1983, p. 140.

[2] Quoted in Wes Granberg-Michaelson, "The Authorship of Life", *Sojourners*, June–July, 1983, p. 18f.

[3] Article in *Atlanta Constitution*, Oct. 8, 1984, p. 12-A.

Six

[1] Steve Baer, "The Bomb", *CoEvolution Quarterly*, Summer, 1976, p. 80.

[2] Jacques Ellul, "Unbridled Spirit of Cowen,", *Sojourners*, July–August, 1982, p. 15.

Seven

[1] James Robertson, *The Sane Alternative: A Choice of Futures*, (St. Paul, Minnesota. River Basin Publishing Co., 1978), p. 127.

[2] William E. Cane, "Is Anything Sacred", *CoEvolution Quarterly*, summer, 1984, p. 72.

Eight

[1] E. F. Schumacher, *Small is Beautiful: Economics as if People Mattered,* (New York: Harper & Row, 1973), p. 281.

[2] Convocation address given at Maryville College, April 21, 1976.

[3] Roger Walsh, *Staying Alive: The Psychology of Human Survival,* (Boulder, Colorado: Shambhala, 1980), p. 55.

BIBLIOGRAPHY

The purpose of the essays in this book has been to stimulate new patterns of awareness and thought. For further stimulation on the tension between technology and human values, I suggest the following books:

Prologue: Did We Come Here to Laugh or Cry?

Pirsig, Robert M. *Zen and the Art of Motorcycle Maintenance*, New York: Bantam Books, 1974.

Walsh, Roger. *Staying Alive: The Psychology of Human Survival*, Boulder, Colorado: New Science Library, 1984.

Technological Progress and Religious Consciousness

Berry, Wendell. *A Continuous Harmony: Essays Cultural and Agricultural*, New York: Harcourt Brace Jovanovich, 1970.

Capra, Fritjof. *The Turning Point: Science, Society, and the Rising Culture*, New York: Bantam Books, 1982.

Davies, Paul. *God and the New Physics*, New York: Simon and Schuster, 1983.

Ferguson, Marilyn. *The Aquarian Conspiracy: Personal and Social Transformation in the 1980s*, Boston: Houghton Mifflin, 1980.

Florman, Samuel C. *The Existential Pleasures of Engineering*, New York: St. Martin's Press, 1976.

LeGuin, Ursula K. *A Wizard of Earthsea*, New York: Ace Books, 1968.

Myers, Norman. Editor, *Gaia: An Atlas of Planet Management*, Garden City, New York: Anchor Press, 1984.

Norman, Colin. *The God That Limps: Science and Technology in the Eighties*, New York: W. W. Norton, 1981.

Rybczynski, Witold. *Taming the Tiger: The Struggle to Control Technology*, New York: Viking Press, 1983.

The Human Scale: Technology As If People Mattered

Berry, Wendell. *The Unsettling of America: Culture & Agriculture*, New York, Avon Books, 1977.

Cauthen, Kenneth. *The Ethics of Enjoyment: The Christian's Pursuit of Happiness*, Atlanta: John Knox Press, 1975.

Harman, Willis W. *An Incomplete Guide to the Future*, San Francisco: San Francisco Book Company, 1976.

Miller, Walter M. Jr. *A Canticle for Leibowitz*, New York: Bantam Books, 1959.

Roszak, Theodore. *Person/Planet: The Creative Disintegration of Industrial Society*, New York: Anchor Press/Doubleday, 1978.

Sale, Kirkpatrick. *Human Scale*, New York: Coward, McCann & Geoghegan, 1980.

Schumacher, E. F. *Small Is Beautiful. Economics as if People Mattered*, New York: Harper & Row, 1973.

Whatever Happened to Mystery?

Berman, Morris. *The Reenchantment of the World*, New York: Bantam Books, 1984.

Capra, Fritjof. *The Tao of Physics*, New York, Bantam Books, 1975.

Dillard, Annie. *Teaching a Stone to Talk: Expeditions and Encounters*, New York: Harper & Row, 1982.

Eiseley, Loren. *The Immense Journey*, New York: Vintage Books, 1956, 1957.

Jones, Roger S. *Physics as Metaphor*, New York: Meridan, 1982.

Thomas, Lewis. *Late Night Thoughts on Listening to Mahler's Ninth Symphony*, New York: Bantam Books, 1984.

The New Literature: Computers

Brand, Stewart. ed. *Whole Earth Software Catalog*, New York: Quantum Press/Doubleday, 1984.

Brod, Craig. *Technostress: The Human Cost of the Computer Revolution*, New York: Addison-Wesley, 1984.

Burnham, David. *The Rise of the Computer State*, New York: Vintage Books, 1984.

Turkle, Sherry. *The Second Self: Computers and the Human Spirit*, New York: Simon and Schuster, 1984.

Weizenbaum, Joseph. *Computer Power and Human Reason: From Judgment to Calculation*, San Francisco: W. H. Freeman, 1976.

Engineering the Engineer: Technology Turned Inward

Glover, Johathan. *What Sort of People Should There Be?*, New York: Penguin Books, 1984.

Rifkin, Jeremy. *Algeny: A New Word—A New World*, New York: Penguin Books, 1984.

Rorvik, David, *As Man Becomes Machine: The Next Step in Evolution*, New York: Pocket Books, 1970, 1971.

Wade, Nicholas. *The Ultimate Experiment: Man-Made Evolution*, New York: Walker and Company, 1977.

Befriending Mount Everest

Geyer, Alan. *The Idea of Disarmament: Rethinking the Unthinkable,* Elgin, Illinois: Brethren Press, 1982.

Lovins, Armory B. *Soft Energy Paths*, New York: Penguin Books, 1977.

Lovins, Armory B. and L. Hunter Lovins, *Energy/War: Breaking the Nuclear Link*, New York: Harper & Row, 1980.

Schell, Jonathan. *The Abolition*, New York: Alfred A. Knopf, 1984.

—, *The Fate of the Earth*, New York: Alfred A. Knopf, 1982.

Harold Willens, *The Trimtab Factor: How Business Executives Can Help Solve the Nuclear Weapons Crisis*, New York: William Morrow, 1984.

Can the Poor People Get a Robot Too?

Brown, Robert McAfee. *Unexpected News: Reading the Bible with Third World Eyes*, Philadelphia, Westminster Press, 1984.

Nouwen, Henry. *¡Gracias!: A Latin American Journal*, New York, Harper & Row, 1983.

Paton, Alan. *Ah, But Your Land is Beautiful,* New York: Charles Scribner's Sons, 1983.

Schaull, Richard. *Heralds of a New Reformation: The Poor of South and North America,* Maryknoll, New York: Orbis, 1984.

Taylor, John V. *Enough is Enough: A Biblical Call for Moderation in a Consumer-oriented Society,* London: SCM Press, 1977.

Inventing the Future

Capra, Fritjof and Charlene Spretnak, *Green Politics: The Global Promise*, New York: E. P. Dutton, 1984.

Cetron, Marvin and Thomas O'Toole, *Encounters with the Future: A Forecast of Life into the 21st Century*, New York: McGraw Hill, 1983.

Hawken, Paul, James Oglivy and Peter Schwartz, *Seven Tomorrows: Toward a Voluntary History*, New York: Bantam Books, 1982.

Naisbitt, John. *Megatrends: Ten New Directions Transforming Our Lives*, New York: Warner Books, 1982.

Robertson, James. *The Sane Alternative: A Choice of Futures*, St. Paul, Minnesota: River Basin Publishing Company, 1979.

Toffler, Alvin. *The Third Wave*, New York: William Morrow and Company, 1980.

von Oech, Roger. *A Whack on the Side of the Head*, New York: Warner Books, 1983.

Wallis, Jim. *Agenda for Biblical People*, New York: Harper & Row, 1976, 1984.

Postscript: Are We Dying or Being Born?

Hoban, Russell. *Riddley Walker*, New York, Summit Books, 1980.

DATE DUE

DEMCO